ANCHOR
BOOKS

# *A Story To Share*

Edited by

Steve Twelvetree

First published in Great Britain in 2004 by
ANCHOR BOOKS
Remus House,
Coltsfoot Drive,
Peterborough, PE2 9JX
Telephone  (01733) 898102

SB ISBN 1 84418 298 3

# *FOREWORD*

Anchor Books is a small press, established in 1992, with the aim of promoting readable poetry to as wide an audience as possible.

We hope to establish an outlet for writers of poetry who may have struggled to see their work in print.

The poems presented here have been selected from many entries, and as always editing proved to be a difficult task.

I trust this selection will delight and please the authors and all those who enjoy reading poetry.

Steve Twelvetree
Editor

# CONTENTS

## IN MY DREAMS

Today I woke up with a start,
I had such a pain in my heart.
What caused it I don't know?
But my tears began to flow.

My dream had seemed so real,
The images I could still feel.
My emotions were running high,
I wanted to leap into the sky.

Suddenly I'm doubled up with mirth,
Now I've come back down to earth.
Nothing exciting happens to me,
What if my dreams become reality?

I would enjoy being Lady Susanna,
Giving orders in a haughty manner.
Every week I'd have dinner parties,
The guests would only eat Smarties.

I'd have servants to grant my every whim,
With a swimming pool so I could swim.
Gardeners to tend everything that grows,
Especially my favourite flower the rose.

Still it's no use dreaming my life away,
To get to work I must be on my way.
I clean for Lady Susanna you see,
She always says she relies on me.

*Rosemary Davies*

## MY DAD

Looking after my old *dad*
Discovering strength I never knew I had
His life seems bad for him right now
I am trying to help but I don't know how
He cannot look after himself anymore
I have tried to help him more and more
Having no time to spare for myself
Not spending much time with anyone else
The days are very long for him that is true
For me there is always so much to do
Doing the washing, cleaning and shopping
And he is getting tired and is doing nothing
The rest of the family are missing me so much
I miss them too but we keep in touch
It's not his fault he is so ill
So back I go to him like I always will

I cannot change what he is used to
He keeps his eye on me whatever I do
I would like to be able to have a choice
To have more freedom would be nice
Doing the housework every day
Not changing anything in any way
Not even able to move a picture frame
Same routine always the same
Changing furniture, curtains too
Is what I really would like to do
They are fine says he, leave them alone
They are okay for me, I am on my own
Same dinners day after day every week
Never indulging in a special treat

Can I cope with all his needs
Day after day trying to please
He is my dad and does need help
I must try and not think of myself

*Ziggybeans*

# GREAT PAN

Once omnipresent in ancient minds,
Now 'myth and legend' we leave behind.
By forgetting them with such success,
We vanquish all, God and Goddess.

His lustfulness was driven out,
'Ere Rome's Priapus walked about.
God degraded to mammal man,
Brought down by us, great fallen Pan.

Cast aside from Dionysus' throne,
Became by name Beast Master known.
A God transformed to lesser man,
Now dead to love, great fallen Pan.

Louring brow, with thoughts perplexing,
Sinews taut, eyes staring hexing.
Yet while Beast Master uneasily sleeps,
In dream world hermaphrodite creeps.

It speaks to him in his stygian mood,
Ambrosia, nectar, come eat your food.
Mankind remembers, you have been lifted,
A sexless thing, I salute one so gifted!

Son of Hermes rejoice! For now,
Nymphs Pitys and Syrinx both kiss your brow.
Renewed to life, because enough believe,
Back to great, Pan now breathes.

Re-affirmed, his ancient loves,
'Ere ashes were scattered by mourning glove.
With his Satyrs in wood, pine needles and leaves
Arisen Pan, great Pan now breathes.

*Eric Ferris*

## PAST, PRESENT, FUTURE

Here in the pale sunlight, dappled upon the wall
I mouth the words, to the mirror in the hall,
Please let me through the hours to lunch,
Please don't let my body feel another punch.

Let there be no words of accusation and filthy abuse
No look, no sigh, no tear, no word, to make him let loose,
With fists and feet upon my crouching form, his rage
Like a crazed animal that has escaped from his cage.

Please let there be no mockery of the sexual act
The silent acquiescence an unspoken, yet dreadful pact,
The violent violation of a body sorely abused
The pain as the act of love, tears at my flesh, leaving confused;

The sad and lonely frightened mind, that left the body to its fate
Please let him not come home, this monster, the man I love and hate.
Let me not betray by look or gesture anything that could inflame
That madness, that escapes, seemingly without blame,

To inflict the wounds on the body and deep within the mind,
You see he is sick, he cannot help it, he does not mean to be unkind,
But when transfixed I feel the cold, cold steel of the gun at my head,
Oh God, please, please don't let him shoot me, I don't want to be dead.

From the past the images came so I am still reminded
Of a time in my life, when by love I was blinded
Now thankfully in the present, with this poem a token
To take into the future, with eyes wide open.

*Carolina de la Cruz*

# THE OLD FARMHOUSE

The farm with bricks of red was quaint,
Beside a sparkling river stood,
With many barns and fields of wheat,
A line of trees to break the wind.

The winding tracks across meadows,
The songs of birds on summer's air,
Reflected light off far windows,
With wind was dancing through my hair.

The house was old and made of stone,
With barns in need of some repair,
The corrugated sheets now gone,
No bales of hay you stand and stare.

The stables' roof with broken tiles,
And overgrown machinery,
The apple orchard, far off dales,
The damson trees, the bumblebees.

The ageing farmer, smiling wife,
Would talk to those who ventured by,
Their rosy cheeks, a working life,
The smell of cooking, apple pie.

The porch with rows of cider jugs,
And tales of happy times now past,
The harvest, cider drank from mugs,
Alas the time has gone so fast.

The chimney smoke, the burning log,
A scented garden, roses near,
The smiling couple, barking dog,
Recalled the memories so dear.

*David M Walford*

## POND MONSTER

At the age of five, Father told me
Of the drooling beast in the pond by the big oak tree.
He told me of its fiery eyes, big and bold,
And of its sharp, green teeth, filling me with terrors untold.
Its breath so stinking, foul and rancid,
And the stories of the terrible things to children it did.
Lucky for me, safety was had,
Because the terrible monster feared Mum and Dad.
I never got the courage to approach that pond of terror,
Or look at the monster, never, ever, ever.
Now I have a son of my own and I understand fully what my
Father was trying to say,
That children should never venture out near water alone,
Not on any night or day.

*Gary Raymond*

# BONFIRE SURPRISE

At the beginning of November, as Guy Fawkes night drew near
My friends and I were looking forward, to celebrations this year,
We collected wood and old furniture, and made an ugly 'guy',
With the help of 'our parents' we then stacked it all up high,
'Grown ups' would be providing fireworks, hot dogs and potatoes,
Just in case of emergencies, we even had a large water hose.

We boys were adding to the 'pile', while waiting for the dark,
From the middle, we heard a sound, was someone having a 'lark'!
We all stopped in our tracks, alarmed! All looking at each other,
After more spluttering coughs, something emerged from under cover,
As a black nose and beady eyes appeared, we were rooted to the spot,
Then it spoke in a croaky squeak, just what had we got?

Jumping back in surprise, as it crossly began to tell us off!
'Now you've woken me up! How dare you stand and scoff!'
We said that we were sorry, 'on our knees for a closer look',
Explaining that if it slept there, it would surely 'cook',
Horror crept across its face, its whole body began to shake,
But I need to hibernate for winter, in spring I shall awake.

Then it dawned upon us, this scared creature was a 'hedgehog',
We must find you another bed, I answered, now sitting all agog,
Rescuing one of the boxes, we packed it with grass and straw,
Quickly it crept inside, a happy smile now on its face it wore,
We took it to the local allotments, and found it a warm safe place,
And agreeing to keep it our secret, back to the bonfire we did race.

*Glenice Siddall*

## WAITING

You have a problem deep inside your mind
People ignore you, they are cruel and unkind
You turn to doctors, psychiatrists and more
You're not sure where you are going or if you've been there before
Have a seat in the waiting room, it's just over there that way
How many hours of the week do you spend each day
Sitting, listening for a door to open, it's your turn
Depression and pain when it's freedom you yearn
Waiting, watching, thinking, locked in despair
Hoping for a miracle that somebody might care
You know each corner, each cobweb, each book
You know every mark on the drab coat hook
Clock ticking on a wall each different each the same
Slowly eating away your life as you play the waiting game
Are you a number, are you a name, or are you just a freak
Will you be who used to be or will you stay timid and meek
Each time you sit in the same chair, somehow feels it's yours
Much less lonely than sitting just indoors
But waiting, waiting every day, sadness sweeps your mind
It never used to be this way now life is just unkind
But then the door opens, you're called, it's your time now
They try their best to help you work out why and how
You leave once more the waiting done until from sleep you rise
When once more you have appointments, once more you look
                                                through eyes
That see the dullness waiting brings but also cling to hope
That one day you can undo the noose, one day let out the rope
So you persevere, you sit upon the chair that has your name
Waiting ever waiting for your mind to once more be sane.

*Sue Starling*

## THE STORY OF FOURTH WISE MAN

I tell a tale of long ago about three wise men on camels go, to follow the
shining star so bright, and meet with Jesus born that night.
They offered gifts of gold, frankincense and myrrh to honour this baby
just born on Earth.
But on this very special night, another man rode filled with delight
This man a sheikh, a wealthy man left his harem and his wives to travel
the desert mile after mile, with train of camel, servants too, to herald the
infant nearly due.
Sadly things went wrong, they lost their way, a sandstorm too came into
play, and servants missed their families, some were feeling very sick,
asked their master could they quit. The bright star had left the sky;
they'd missed his birth by many miles.
Sheikh still mindful of his quest said, 'I would remain and rest awhile,
go back to your homeland it's many miles.
Take with you some goods and camels; just leave with me what I can
manage.'
So Sheikh Abdul as was his name, was left alone to travel on and seek
out the place our Lord had gone.
When he in Bethlehem arrived, tired and weary all money spent on
other people with good intent.
Many good deeds he did on the way, helping others and not for pay.
Years began to take their toll, he now must rest could not go on.
Meeting Jesus seemed not to be, so he prayed that night to God above;
and thanked him for the Saviour's love.
That very night in soft moonlight, he did see Jesus standing there. His
halo lit up all around and marked the place his body found. Jesus found
him dying there, with gentle voice he spoke to him.
'All my work you have done, now is the time for you to come.'
So sweet the smile on Abdul's face, he'd met his master filled
                                                    with grace.

*Joan Prentice*

## STREET MUSICIAN

We came across an old man, sitting cross-legged on the ground,
He played an old, battered violin, but oh what treasure we had found!
The music poured out so delightful and pure, as if straight from Heaven,
What a rare and unexpected gift this man had been given.
His face reflected all the joy and emotion that he felt,
Carried away, living the notes, any hearts he would melt.
The music floated on the air, a celestial aura around,
The place was hushed, all movement stopped, no one wanted to
                                             make a sound,
When the piece was finished, this master of the art,
I asked him why he played on the street, instead of the theatre a part?
'I've been there,' he said, 'but got no satisfaction
From the rich and privileged, snobbish faction,
God gave me this talent to share with all,
That's why I sit with my back to this wall
And play my music from the depth of my being,
It's not any old tramp that you're seeing.
I once was renowned and hailed as a master
But it was peace and beauty on the innocent face I was after,
I need to share, with ordinary people, who can appreciate this gift,
To transform them for a few moments and give their lives a lift,
*That's* why I sit here day after day -
And hope that I help them in some small way.
We are told 'not to hide our light under a bushel' so I let it shine,
You have your mission in life - this is mine!'

*Doris I Livesey*

## THE SIKH AT THE BUS STOP

'Is this the stop for London?'
'Yes, it is - I'm going there myself.'
The handsome Sikh, dressed all in white,
Smiled, and his eyes were deep and dark.
Swirls of sweet eastern perfume wafted
Around us, as we spoke.
'I came to see my sister off,' I said
And this began our conversation.

We talked and talked.
We spoke about the children of the world
And how we all are one.
We had so much to say and share -
There was an urgent feeling in the air - and time was short.
And yet, time did not exist for us just then.
The bus forgotten, we put the world to rights.
A few moments of complete at-onement
With another human being, and two minds as one,
And the minutes passed without our knowledge.

Suddenly, the bus drew up, my sister climbed aboard.
The Sikh followed, then he turned and said,
'It was so wonderful to talk to you.'
'Yes, I enjoyed it so much too.'
He took a few more steps, and turned again
To smile and wave goodbye.
'Take care, God bless,' we said,
And so it was - the bus had gone . . .

Our bodies had to go a different way -
But our souls were as one on this lovely summer's day.

*Betty Farajallah*

## FISHERMAN

Whilst looking round a garden store
Some goldfish I espied,
All swimming in a lovely pond
With plants around the side.
As I was gazing quite absorbed,
An older man approached me.
He murmured, 'I sure like these carp,
A fisherman I used to be.
When in my youth I'd cast a line
In many a lake and stream.
Trout I've caught and salmon too,
Also I've fished for bream.
But I'm not a cruel fellow.
I just loved to get a bite,
Then I took the hook out of its jaws
And watched it swim in flight.'
I wonder how the fish felt
With its mouth spiked on a hook,
Then thrown back in the river . . .
Another one for the book?
If I should be an angler,
I'd sit beneath the trees
And idly watch the dragonflies
Floating brightly on the breeze.
I'd linger by the ripples
Watch the fishes gliding there,
Admire the flash of silver gleam,
Just simply stand and stare.
An angler I could never be,
I'd feel the fishes' pain.
I couldn't ply with rod and line
Then toss them back again.

*E Balmain*

# WHEN AS A BOY AND OF A CLOCK

When as a boy, I used to be contented, though 'twere sad,
For we, albeit, were at war, and was wi'out my dad.
But, as it were, I didn't know no other life as then -
Messing around wi' catapults, or build a gangland den.

My brother, and my sister too, were equally as me.
Together, mother marvelled at us 'understanding' three.
We'd make a mockery of muck, fain ev'ryday I fear.
Whence each of us was dealt the same - a clip around the ear.

From morning until night we'd play, and oft' times into scrapes.
O'er hill and dale, a tribe of us excitedly would traipse.
Oft' falling into ponds and pits, wi' tadpoles in our socks,
Or falling into nettlebeds, thence soothing sores wi' 'docks'.

By and large 'twere happy days, and ignorance was bliss,
Whence paper-chasing through the fields, my brother, me, and sis.
Just doing what we chose to do, and when, and where, and how,
Where truth-and-dare were commonplace, as common as the cow.

Oh how we used to chance our luck when scrumping season loomed,
We'd fearlessly our pockets fill, when as the farmer 'boomed'.
And apples then were bunged about - distasteful ones I guess,
Bespattering the streets and greens in one unholy mess.

The village clock was stopped by one half-eaten apple-core.
I can remember it quite well, we gasped - we wasn't sure.
The missile didst contrive to wedge right underneath the hand,
Whereby the minutes ebbed away, to stutter, thence to stand.

In Sunday school the vicar spoke about the awful 'sin' -
That just a few unruly souls had put the parish in.
He asked questions, and begat a statutory moue,
And all was quiet as the clock, well, what was one to do?

Our mums and dads were definite, it wasn't their offspring,
And 'twas a blessing in disguise to hear the bell - not ring.
So silence through the village reigned, until the fateful day -
When they wound up the clock again, and took the chore away.

*Derek Haskett-Jones*

# THE COLOUR!

What is the colour of your soul
When you go to sleep and die?
What colour are the tears you shed
When heartache makes you cry?

What colour is your skin
When it is burned with a fire?
What colour is the doctors that help
To heal your hurt's desire?

Did you know our skin
Will only live if we have a soul?
It keeps our working parts together
So our life can become whole!

What colour is a life without a soul?
What colour is then our skin?
It rots away to the colour black,
Try to live without racist sin!

***Janet Brook***

## THE DOG ROSE

The dog rose planted at the tree
In memory of Molly's tragedy.
It was March nineteen forty-three
We planted the dog rose John and me.
Snow still lay thick upon the ground
Crying and sobbing the only sound.
Then we heard the planes overhead
There had been no siren John said.
We stood beneath the bare leaf tree
There was need to run or flee
Only sorrow felt by John and me.
Then the years just rolled by
Moving north was the reason why,
Never forgotten was Molly's tree.
Or the dog rose planted in forty-three
Decades would pass before I'd see,
The snow-white dog rose on the tree.
I stood alone and tears fell
Lovely Molly I remembered well.
John and I were parted long ago
No idea where he is anymore.
With sadness I write my rhyme
Molly died at the wrong time,
That tragedy was John's and mine.
As no one else seemed to care
Nor our sorrow did they share.
It was a scandal that was all
Now I watch as the petals fall.
I put my pen and pad away
Too much sorrow for me to stay.
Scent of the dog rose in the air
Life for dear Molly was not fair.

*Mary Long*

# BOROMIR'S DEMISE

Searching evil eye probes his muddied mind with urgent need
soft, whispered promises, dark receiver feeding basic human greed
tempting the stoutest foe with shadowed glimpse of gloried lust
stirring forgotten memories, lost legions turned to crumbled dust
invading dreams, hinting a return to Gondor's golden reign
mental prompting controls his purpose, itching to reclaim Isildur's bane
mortal muscle wrestling hobbit, seizing Frodo of the Shire
Boromir's tormented soul struggling against the demon's inner fire
pinning Frodo to the ground, testing barriers, forcing loyalty apart
vanished ring-bearer alerting darkness, releasing goodness
from the heart
Boromir's scream of anguish over committed deed, 'Friend forgive me.'
Pippin and Merry, hobbits caught in descending swarm of blackest sea
white hand of Saruman glows upon evil's black spawned skin
genetic collection given life, amalgamation of every mortal sin
regretful Boromir sounds the horn of Gondor, facing festered foes
standing firm, calling upon the strength of ancestral woes
flashing blade, flailing boot, piling stinking corpses all around
reeking stench of death, reddening stain spreads blood-filled ground
first black-feathered shaft, piercing pause in desperate final glory
Uruk-hai release arrow after arrow, ending Boromir's fateful story
hero warrior slumps upon his knees, wearing killer's lethal deed
Aragorn answers fading echo, Boromir's silent horn with urgent need
sadness tightens grip upon his heart, forlorn figure's fading light
brave Boromir clutches broken blade, surrounded by Saruman's blight
striding scattered bodies, Aragorn kneels to hear his dying breath
denying his words of failure, selfless sacrifice soul's
redemption in death
arriving late upon the scene, Legolas and Gimli abandon stealthy course
collecting shield, helm and sword from Isengard's defeated force
honouring Boromir's final journey with symbols of the enemy's might
casting adrift his body, wooden boat follows Gondor's river flight

*Paul Birkitt*

## Every Mother's Nightmare

Pregnancy time has gone its full length
The tired mum is resting after baby's first breath
Baby's asleep in its own little bed
And all is serene after baby's been fed

But evil is lurking and making its plan
'I want a baby and I'll steal if I can'
Are the thoughts of the woman watching the scene
Ready to carry out this thought so obscene

Security cameras fixed on the walls
In entrances, wards and communication halls
None will deter this desperate thief
Nor cause her to think of the new mum's great grief

Like a hawk hovering over its prey
The snatcher then pounces and the baby's away
Routine checks by staff discover the theft
The mother when told is with grief so bereft

In most cases like this there is a happier ending
Mother and baby reunited restarting their bonding
But forever stuck in the mind of the mother
Will be the thought of attempt another.

*Archie Livingstone*

## FROM PTERODACTYL TO CONCORDE: BOTH BEAUTY AND THE BEAST OF TEENAGE WOMAN UNFURLED

I'm what you may call an intellectual hard working girl;
And there are lots of them about!
I like to study hard and play hard too, of that there is no doubt,
I'm studying hard at uni' for I want to make top grade:
In philosophy and anthropology I know I've got things made.
Some say I've got an old head on young shoulders,
But that won't pay my fees:
In fact I'm quite fun-loving too in life's putting on
and taking off strip-tease.
Though I'm only nineteen summers, I know only too well
what lies ahead:
And to make it to the top I know it will be hard and not a feather bed.
When I saw the last Concorde gracefully coming down to land;
The vision of what I witnessed made me think of a primeval
pterodactyl,
Extinct yet with awesome incandescent beauty planned.
A mighty beast roaring across some wild primeval world:
The old and the new combined in a parallel universe unfurled.
All such joys and wonders are open to me as a twenty-first century
fiery, feisty babe;
The best of two centuries now open wide to me, wide-eyed winsome
and ready to rave,
Ready to unlease the screaming, wild wanton woman that's in me:
Yet sophisticated like the Concorde the best of the old and new century.
For at night I perform totally nude in a twilight town show:
I'm known as the Uni Teenage Queen Lap Dancer and let
everything go.
The regular customers know I'm a Fresher student boosting my grant:
To aid my top-up allowance I take off my top and bottoms:
there's no way that I can't!
For I've an old head on young teenage shoulders that is true:
But I've also got a shapely figure and don't mind everyone
enjoying the exquisite nude view.

As I slip off my ribbon of a thong and gyrate wildly naked around:
I'm not only enjoying my own exciting performing, I'm earning an
extra grant, no G-strings attached, pound.
I shake my buxom booty in a non-stop motion of bare bottom bouncing,
rolling and wiggling;
Like a throw back to a wild rampant cave girl, teasing her caveman
with animal-like wriggling.
But when I go back to uni' I'm always totally demure:
I put on my seriously studious face and costume as I walk sedately
through the door.
To celebrate the fact that I enjoy the best of both worlds
On one bare bottom cheek I've got a tattoo of the sleek beauty of
Concorde,
And on the other, I have my wild side exposed, with a tattoo
of a primeval pterodactyl, exquisitely unfurled!

*Lucinda-Gwendoline Tavistock Farmer Jones*

## UNCLE SAM (SAMMY)

I speak with words not spoken.
I am strong never to be broken.
In my room my books abound.
I cannot hear a sound.
I have a brother like no other.
He's very good and so he should.
I see a picture of Sammy in the front room.
He was taken much too soon.
He had on a cap and a lovely smile.
I stayed and looked at him for a while,
And on to the King's Park I loved best of all.
I didn't hear you call.
I am in the springtime of my childhood years
And I know nothing about so many fears.
So here I am. So my Uncle Sam
Here I am.

*Lyn Fitzpatrick*

## THE REVOLUTIONARY

There was once a man who spread God's glory -
A humble carpenter's son;
He knew the answers to all our problems -
He didn't please everyone!
So they put Him to death
And with His last breath
He told a killer He'd meet him in Heaven -
His message was love and the sinner forgiven;
That didn't go down with those ancient folk -
In our everyday world it's merely a joke.

*Leo Taylor*

# THE LOST OTTER

*(Based on the chapter 'A Piper At The Gates Of Dawn'*
*from 'The Wind In The Willows' by Kenneth Graham)*

Along the reedy river bank
Where sunlit ripples lapped the sedge,
Clustered gleams of green reflections
Quivered at the water's edge.

The hush of twilight had begun
To muffle nature's strident calls,
And in the distance could be heard
The muted splash of waterfalls.

Two figures sailed their little barque,
Intent upon their chosen quest
To find an otter which had strayed,
Leaving parents sorely stressed.

Gliding on the silvered lake
Towards a strange, enchanted isle,
They saw a pale, ethereal light,
Tempting them to stay awhile.

From swirling mists the great god, Pan,
Secure in his awesome power,
Commanded their obedience,
And bade them share this magic hour.

Rat and Mole, wide-eyed with wonder,
Watched the otter as he slept,
Nestling near the cloven hooves
Of Pan whose vigil had been kept.

Then the kindly demi-god
Vanished like a whiff of smoke,
Leaving them to wait and ponder
Till the sleeping otter woke.

Across the water came a whisper
Carried on the dancing breeze,
And with it sweet forgetfulness
Of golden moments such as these.

*Celia G Thomas*

## BOBBIE'S STORY

'How are you my dear?' says a voice from the right,
The cataract eyes view the misty daylight.
'You'll be wanting your brekkies,' echoes the voice,
'Is it toast, flakes or porridge? You have the choice.'
Bobbie surveys the nursing home door,
Awake from her dreams of walking the moor.
Remembering the days when with wind in her hair
And cheeks full of roses she strode without care.
Recalling with pride, when as a young bride,
She would measure the ebb and the flow of the tide,
From her home on the cliffs, abutting the sea
She was happy and loved, and bountifully free.
'Tea or coffee my dear?' from a voice at the rear,
No answer from Bobbie, she does not want to hear.
She's away with her thoughts of being up with the dawn
Making the scones for cream teas on the lawn.
Brought back to the present to wipe away tears,
She feels everyone of her ninety-eight years,
Oh for one moment to go back in time,
Would be for this lady, truly sublime.

*Doreen P Damsell*

# UNDER PRESSURE

I was cooking a stew one day
My friend on the phone rang to say,
'Could we have a little chat?'
I was all for a bit of that.

We chatted for quite a while
I forgot the stew was on the boil,
There was an almighty crash
Pressure cooker had blown with a bash.

My friend on the phone could hear it too
The ceiling was now covered with stew,
It was dripping on the floor
A mess to clean up - what a bore.

My daughter was trying on something new
Didn't know about the stew,
Thought a train had come through the house
Screamed as if she'd seen a mouse.

The dog sat trembling in his box
He couldn't get out, the door was locked.
He was so pleased when I opened the door
The hot stew was dripping on his paw.

My husband came home from work
Didn't know what in the house lurked
'Where's my dinner?' he said without a care.
'It's on the ceiling right up there.'

It took so long to scrub the floor
Stuck like glue to the ceiling and door.
I won't use a pressure cooker again
Couldn't stand the stress and strain.

*Margaret Marston*

# A Traveller's Tale

'Follow me,' said the sprightly elf. 'Come into the woods, there's a
message pinned upon the door of the great magician, Edmund Boar.'

'Follow you? Whatever for? This is the way I wish to go, for I fear
daylight's fading, my eyelids are getting heavy, besides I've no wish to
see the door.'

'Not even for a penny?' asked the little fellow.

'Not even for a penny, indeed, I have plenty.'

'Please sir, I know the day is ending, the moon is climbing high. The
sun is slipping over the mountains to wish the day goodbye. If you
would just grant me a moment, the message may be worthwhile.'

'Well little elf you persistent fellow, show me then the door so I can be
on my way once more.'

Beneath a rambling hedge they stood, where pinned upon a red door
was indeed a message written by Edmund Boar.
And this is what it said . . .

This message here that you can see was meant only for you to read, if
you are a certain travelling man whose heart is honest, good and glad.

The traveller laughed, 'It's surely not I, this message could be meant
for any guy.'

'Go on, go on,' said the excited elf, 'knock on the door, be let in, for
those called upon by Edmund Boar can expect a gift of some sort.'

The door was opened by a gentle old man, who bid them enter,
'Welcome, welcome my dear man. Come into my parlour, we will have
jam, toast and tea, all sorts of dishes to tempt you, if you please.'

'For what do owe this honour? I am no one special which you can
plainly see, my clothes are dirty, torn and old, my hat is rimless,
my shoes are worn.

The magician replied through a mouthful of cheese, 'It's the little people you have pleased. You treat their woods with respect, never leave any mess, you claim to always have plenty yet your purse is always empty. They gave me this message for you to receive, go to the place of the cherry tree. There's gold and silver awaiting you there, a gift, a present because you cared.'

*Jane Margaret Isaac*

## AT BLENHEIM PALACE 22.06.2001

A tiny silver speck
Way, way up in the sky,
I can't imagine how high?
Suddenly like cotton threads
Appearing from this speck,
I counted twelve in all,
They floated down,
The start of a magnificent display
By the RAF Falcons.
What a thrill for us watching,
Enthralled by this spectacle
On this perfect summer's day.
Entertained by various bands
We three ex Wrens enjoying every minute
With a glass of wine, lovely food,
What a wonderful picnic,
A dream come true.
Memories of service days
On this special occasion
At Blenheim Palace, Oxfordshire,
In aid of SSA Forces Charities.

*J Nicoll*

## JUSTICE?

Today he had to take the stand
In court, expounding awkward facts
That helped condemn, along with clues
That other experts had revealed,
A lass for whom he felt it would
Suffice to reprimand alone.
In self-defence she went too far
In stabbing brute with carving knife.
But his attack on her, and rape,
Would turn a saint to crime. He got
What he deserved. But law must take
Its course it seems, as faded judge
With jaded mind, and secret lust
For pretty woman in the dock,
Decides she must be sent to jail
For many years for killing man
He saw as self in fancy's dream.

*Henry Disney*

## THE BARGEMAN

'This place with its uncanny atmosphere
all people must avoid at Hallowe'en.
More fraught with danger than a lit-up town.
Remember last year? Those who dared to stay here
all night long? At dawn, to show where they'd been
trampled grass, and prints in mud leading down
to the stream's edge. In vain we searched this wood.
How or why they vanished none understood . . .

Perhaps like us they heard a raven caw.
Under darkening skies, here shadows glide.
Last Hallowe'en, what more than this was seen?
Who but the dread Bargeman steering slow,
moonlight revealing where the fishes slide.
A watervole tried to remain unseen . . .
. . . wild creatures know what his journey might mean
. . . why an owl flaps away . . . why the winds keen.

From a near battlefield long forgotten
. . . a churchyard . . . standing stones . . . mound grassy green
. . . drifted wraiths . . . spectres . . . the night's walking dead
who watched the bargeman take aboard those men.
Wild creatures he ignored, seen or unseen
and apparitions whose souls were long fled.
He preferred the passengers seized instead
to carry to distant realms of the dead.

We need to hurry from this eerie place.
This eve no one will vanish without trace.'

*Chris Creedon*

# A NIGHT TO REMEMBER

No military target - Exeter!
So with the siren's barb
we quickly rose from sleep and dressed
in superficial garb.
But soon the bombers streaked across
and rent the midnight sky,
their bombs rained down on house and home
to shatter, crucify!
When, suddenly the sky was filled
with lights a thousandfold -
incendiaries to burn it down
our college's stronghold.
Just then a cry, 'The chapel roof.'
'Three lengths of hose,' I cried,
a burning bomb was lodged up there,
a source of fire espied.
Soon it was out. The water failed,
a bomb had hit its track;
we raced across the open road
to drag the power pumps back.
We dived for cover as a bomb
blew up our swimming pool
and left a puddle in the hole
to miss the college school.
The firemen then took over as
St Luke's began to burn:
Two hundred student teachers lost
their everything in turn.
　　They sadly caught their trains back home
　　in covered nightwear, ash and foam.

*Owen Edwards*

## SLEEP TIME

Here in my bed
And very near to sleep
A bedtime story
Promise not to peep,
Is it wizards, witches
Or maybe queens and kings,
Fairies from the garden
One or two that sing?
I see we've gnomes and goblins
But only if I'm sleeping,
Sleeping instant delve.

*Michael D Bedford*

# MEETING AGAIN

I remember it like it was only yesterday
Hiding behind the old garden shed in the sun
Waiting for him to walk down the path
Fearful, yet shy and confused of my feelings.

He arrived with luggage in hand
Cases, bags and boxes galore
Placing them carefully in a large pile
Before he knocked firmly on the glass door.

Tall and handsome in his dark uniform
His polished buttons shone in the morning sun
His eyes sparkled and laughed around the garden
But behind his beard hid a scary grin.

I sneaked to the pile so neatly stacked
And saw a white dog that barked and walked
Presents from lands so far away
Oh look there's a koala bear! Is that for me?

I was six years old when I last saw him
Before he left again to travel the world
In an hour's time we'll catch up on our years apart
Will he still like his little sister after thirty years?

### *Joy Horne*

# LAST SONG FROM AMSTERDAM

The boy from Oklahoma
Was fine-boned and sensitive.
He grew to be 'Jack Lord' handsome
And his misty, beguiling trumpet
Had females in a swoon.

*I fall in love too easily . . .*

He kept a fragile singing voice
On the far horizon, which
Carried on a soft breeze
Into the whirlpool of emotion.

*My funny Valentine . . .*

The double 'd' dragged him
Up and down the scale,
But the pain was always there -
Hanging on the stave.

*Let's get lost . . .*

After that long night, he drifted
Away from the melody, out through
A hotel window in Amsterdam,
Onto the pavement below.

Chet Baker is gone,
But his music lives on
And everything is cool, man.

**Cavan Magner**

## JUST A HICCUP

Everywhere we used to see her bobbin here and there
No matter if the wind did blow, if it was wet or fair
So many tasks Yvonne would do by helping on the farm
As well as household duties she would keep the sheep from harm
Take care of cows and little lambs with not a sign of tension
Keep villagers supplied with stamps and not give it a mention
But that was all before the feet became a pressing problem
With causing pain and lots of moans by growing each a bunion
No trouble for a surgeon this, he fixed them with a knife
But our Yvonne is living now a very different life
No more the morning walk at dawn to check the fields and hutches
She hobbles round the sitting room upon a pair of crutches
Reliant on her family she's feeling very restless
Not liking daytime telly and the knowledge that she's helpless
So down the lane she sails once more to get some nice fresh air
But looking somewhat different perching in her new wheelchair
Accepting greetings from all sides, a big smile on her face
With ten pink toes just peeping out of bandages and tape
A few more weeks of sitting down and limping and the like
And she'll be back as we all know her - riding on her bike.

*Dorothy Blakeman*

# ALL'S WELL THAT ENDS WELL

*It goes like this . . .*

She doesn't sit by him in the pub
Or talk to him at the party

Their eyes don't meet across a crowded room
They do not get stuck in a lift together

She doesn't come to see his room for rent
Or sign up to the same evening course

She doesn't bump into him in the aisle
Right by the organic food

She doesn't hear him on empty nights
Playing songs having turned out the lights

She doesn't read his ad in the paper
Never hears his voice on the phone

*And furthermore . . .*

She doesn't work where he works
Walk where he walks
Speak when he's listening
Or hear when he talks

She doesn't notice the book
He reads in the park
Or the postcard from Columbia
Used as a bookmark

She doesn't dance at the festival
Laugh at the play
Sing at the gig
Or shout at the game

She doesn't sail on the boat
Ride on the train
Cruise in the coach
Or fly in the plane

Their sisters aren't friends
Brothers aren't friends
Parents aren't friends
Their friends aren't friends

*But . . .*

Once, she hailed a taxi
And left him standing
Twenty yards
Down the road

And then, they met in a club
And she couldn't hear
What he was saying but . . .
The music was too loud

All's well that ends well.

**Tim Wilson**

## DEEP SEA DIVER

I started off in Brighton in a café by the sea,
I left there with some change from a bacon roll with tea.
I travelled then to London where I changed hands on a bus,
The driver had no change you see so I seemed to cause a fuss.
I finished in the depot where I found some other friends,
I was counted at the bank which is where my story ends.
It's quite a hectic life and I don't know how I cope,
The stresses and the strains of an English five pound note.

*Nicola Healey*

## A BASKET OF FLOWERS FOR THE PRINCESS

The garden fête took place in June
A princess came to open it
A two-year-old must play her part
With a basket of flowers quite soon.

For several weeks she'd learned what to say
'A basket of flowers for the princess.' The day
The princess came to open the fête
She stood erect to receive her bouquet.

The small girl advanced and had her say
She said her words quite perfectly
The princess reached to accept her gift
Which small girl clutched tight and said, 'No way.'

Quick as a flash the princess dug
Deep inside her black dolly bag
And brought out a box of Edinburgh rock
They made fair exchange. Now no need to cry

Instead the end was a friendly hug.

*Dolly Harmer*

## LITTLE BECKY

Becky sobbed ceaselessly, 'You're too little,' cried her big brothers,
'you just can't play.'
I smiled as I heard great grandpa cough 'um', he would always
start a story this way.
He started, 'If I remember, long ago there was a grand garden in
a corner quite overgrown,
There was a tatty old garden shed standing all alone.'
Becky stopped her smiling and sat upon his knee
With her great big eyes her look was more a plea,
So on he went to tell her of a sad little garden trowel
Oh how the other tools would laugh, taunt her and howl,
'You're so very tiny, what's the good of you?'
Snooty lawnmower dusting his blades said, 'This is such a to do.'
Big fork was very bossy and snapped, 'I can dig down deep.'
Spade pointed out she too could shovel great big heaps.
Rake called, 'Look at me, in autumn I am just a must.'
The stiff garden broom haughtily sneered, 'Well I sweep away
all the dust.'
Wheelbarrow squeaked, 'You all need me to fetch and carry from
the work you do.'
'But I am far the strongest,' bellowed mighty roller, 'than any
one of you.'
From a dark corner hissed the hose, 'Yes, but who waters the garden in
the summer sun?'
'So what good are you?' they all laughed, and jeered, 'you're such
a little one.'
All at once the door swung open, 'I am sure I hear voices, oh well
perhaps not,' he sighed.
'Here you are my trusty friend,' and handed little trowel to a boy
at his side.
'Now you take very good care of it, it's been with me all my
gardening life.
Hurry along now, plant your seeds, I'll fetch lemonade from my wife.'
As he was about to turn away, he heard a gasp from inside,

'I really think I am hearing things, a little sit down will do the trick,
I am a little tired.'
'The shed's still quite broken down, the old tools lie rusting about
But little trowel is still shiny and new, of this I have no doubt.'
Becky jumped from Grandpa's lap, 'Can we plant seeds
Grandpa, please?'
Grandpa's story had made her glad, as I saw her on her knees,
Pleased that she was quite small, just as back so many years, it did
the same for me.
Now in the shed lies a worn out boot, in which Mrs Mouse lives in,
If you are very still at twilight, you will hear a story being told
there within.
'Once upon a time the nasty tools,' and so from there it begins,
Sometimes an old gardener in passing, stops to listen, shakes his head,
mutters, 'No,'
But we know, don't we, what we would hear if down the garden we
should go?

*Susan E Roffey*

# WHOSE HANDBAG?

All the staff was busy, tending to their chores,
I could see them working quietly, from inside the kitchen doors.

Some laying out the tables, another poured a drink,
One was cooking in the kitchen, preparing at the sink.

'Anyone need any help?' I said, not knowing what to do,
'Can I be of help to anyone, assisting one of you?'

'Alright, thank you,' those were the words, on that they all agreed,
Into the kitchen I did roam, my help I thought they'd need.

Everything was simmering; all was quite in hand,
The gravy now was ready in a boiler on a stand.

I thought I'll turn the heat up to make the gravy boil,
Imagine how I panicked to see the gravy spoil.

It poured out from the boiler, in gushes from the top,
Running down the cupboards, on the floor, 'Let's get a mop.'

Well imagine what a shock we had as we peered onto the ground,
As someone's handbag lay there, suede and grey and round.

The gravy filled the handbag, we thought what could we do?
I asked the staff, with bag in hand, 'Does this belong to you?'

No one claimed the handbag, so who had left it there?
Whoever it belonged to just didn't seem to care.

We never found who owned it, it didn't have a tag,
You can order food in baskets, now gravy in a bag.

*Betty Hattersley*

## MOTORWAY MADNESS

I slipped on smoothly and found
My place in the central reservation.
There was a Merc in front and an Astra behind
And a Transit in the inside position.
Boy Beemer raced by a ton or more
And the order was right on expectation.

The Transit signalled right which then meant
A move - quick nip into the outside lane.
The Astra tailed me over and so we both
Got by white van man nice and clean.
But the Merc was hemmed - he couldn't overtake
So that's the order blown up again.

The Merc braked hard as he moved to the left and
Put his foot down to burn up the inside.
That meant me and the Astra were left
High and dry and I then couldn't decide
Should I move back inside or stay where I was?
What's the order when the rules are aside?

I moved to the left as the Merc moved to the right
As the Beemer had to slam on his brakes.
And the Astra behind really hadn't a chance
As we swerved to avoid fatal mistakes.
It's motorway madness and it's just the thing
For order pecking away
And the shakes.

*Trudy Valentine*

## HAUNTED PUB SESTINA

There is a pub on the road to the coast
That specialises in a nice Sunday roast,
They advertise every week in the 'Post',
That this is the pub whose meals are the most,
And not only that, but they also can boast
That this pub is haunted by a resident ghost.

So if you should fancy hunting for a ghost,
Drop into that pub as you head for the coast,
And then you will find out if it's just a boast,
But you will have a chance then to sample their roast,
The chance to assess if their meals are the most.
And live up to their weekly ad in the 'Post'

The thing that they mention each week in the 'Post',
Is the bygone days past of their historic ghost,
You never know, you may be luckier than most,
Cos many drop in on their way to the coast,
If you'd like to see him, drop in for a roast,
You might find their spectre is more than a boast.

To give you the low-down on their spectral boast,
A long time before someone founded the 'Post',
That pub was renowned for its fine Sunday roast,
A highwayman working that road to the coast,
Frequented that pub quite a bit more than most,
Until he was hanged and came back as a ghost.

If you take more interest in spirits than most,
And want to see something of which you can boast,
Pop into that pub on the road to the coast,
You'll find all the details you want in the 'Post',
You might just be lucky, you might see the ghost,
But don't let the spectre put you off your roast.

That highwayman so loved his nice Sunday roast,
And they cooked it tender, much nicer than most,
That's how he was caught and turned into a ghost,
Which is why the pub's claim is much more than a boast,
As they say in their weekly advert in the 'Post',
Try the 'Highwayman' pub on the road to the coast.

If you want to boast you've seen a ghost,
Pop in that pub on t' road t' coast,
See t' ad in t' 'Post', their roast's the most.

*Mick Nash*

## BALLAD OF THE WANDERER

Two young folk when first we came
To harvest in the vale,
On summer days, it seemed a game
To share a song and spin a tale.
Then autumn came, and we returned
To city homes apart.
In absence, still the love-fire burned
And glowed in my young heart.
Yes, young forever, I could swear
And strong forever too.
Now I am old, my hair is grey,
There's little I can do.
And she - she lives far-off as well
And sorrows as I do,
Her marriage only brought her hell,
New tears have dimmed her eye.

But blame not me and blame not her -
For we were tricked by time -
Live now, speak swift, do not defer -
So ends my traveller's rhyme.

*Ruth Partington*

# No Smoke Without Fire!

Once there was a dustbin
That was full of human trash:
Of cigars and pipe tobacco,
And cigarettes and ash.

Its owner gave up smoking,
So he said - well, more or less.
Now what a state the dustbin's in -
Cor blimey; what a mess!

Its owner should have burnt the lot,
And given the fire a poking;
He would have, but his garden has
A sign which reads: 'No Smoking!'

*Roger Williams*

## WE SAT DOWN

We lit the candle and sat down.
No power here, just the wind.
There were two of us alone and still
the keeper of the light and me, his pal.
He stroked his beard and prepared his tale:
It was about 3am, the outer door clicked
and up went the latch.
I picked up an axe.
There appeared a man, upright, swarthy
flashing eyes.
Where he stood he dripped and dripped
his clothes were plastered onto him.
I raised my axe thus, ready to defend,
he grabbed my arm, he smelt of blood and rum.
'I mean no harm,' said he.
'A change of clothes, some warming food
and a place to put my head,' as he spoke he bled.
I stoked the fire, and we sat down
he ate, he drank, he bled,
we changed his bandages and clothes.
Now feeling calmer I stayed alert.
It seemed he'd almost drowned, escaping from his
prison irons off convict ship.
I watched him sleep, the colour seeping from
that weathered face.
Come daylight I too had nodded off
and when I awoke, I saw a note
scratched from quill and more red blood:
'Keeper of the light, you have saved a soul tonight.'
Of my pirate there was no sign, if pirate he had been.

I shuddered and moved towards the outer door
opening it, I walked to the cliff.
He lay spread-eagled on the slimy shale, lifeless now.
I sang a dirge: and the sea reclaimed her man!

*F A C*

## THE GATE

One day as I walked along a country lane
I was feeling hopeless, so alone,
When further down the lane I came upon a garden
That was neglected - overgrown.
As I paused, surveying the scene I felt sadness by what I saw,
Nobody seemed to care, once they may have
But obviously not any more.
Just as I was about to move on, I noticed a gate leaning where
Once it stood square,
On closer inspection I could see, that it was in need of urgent repair.

The paint that had adorned it was now fading away,
And the hinge it once swung on was rusty, so it could no longer sway.
Beyond the gate was a path with roses growing on either side,
But sadly to see they stood among weeds which were suffocating
Their pride.
At the end of the path was a cottage, its shutters closed to keep
Out the light,
I felt such affinity with this rundown place,
It seemed to mirror my own plight.

My life was bleak like these surroundings,
And I was finding it hard to bear,
But just as I turned to walk away, I noticed a for sale sign standing
there.
A flicker of interest began to surface but I told myself beware,
I wasn't ready to make decisions - so I knew that I must take care.
I had no doubts at all in my mind that this garden wanted to live,
So I shouldn't take it on, if I wasn't prepared to give.

Was I ready to do that, would I be able to rise above
My bereaved despair?
It's very hard to give to life again when you lose the one for
Whom you care.
But perhaps this place and I was meant to heal moving forward
Side by side,
Fate does sometimes have a way of giving a hand, to help us to survive.
Well a year has passed by since I first saw that gate and the sign,
The shutters now stay open - roses are thriving - and most days -
I feel fine.
As for the gate it has new hinges, fresh paint and easily swings
To and fro.
Which it often does when newly made friends,
Visit with a cheerful hello.

*B Lamus*

## THE FINAL AFFAIR

I'm sick of the heartache, sick of the pain,
Why did you have to do this again?
All those promises, smashed and broken,
Words of love, carelessly spoken.

I'm really sorry I've broken your heart,
Please don't leave me, I don't want us to part.
One more chance, that's all it will take,
If not for me, then for the kids' sake.

No more chances, not this time,
As for the kids, they'll be just fine.
I loved you so much, not enough it seems,
It's finally over, no more dreams.

I've been such a fool, pathetic and weak,
A life without you would be empty and bleak.
I love you so much, believe me I do,
It's always been you and only you.

I've heard it before, the same old line,
Over and over, time after time.
Please just go, leave me alone,
Don't call around, don't even phone.

I'll always love you, but it just won't work,
Doubts and fears will always lurk.
You can see the kids whenever you like,
I'll talk with them, they'll be alright.

A frightening future lies ahead,
A quiet apartment, an empty bed.
What had he done, what had it cost?
His family life suddenly lost.

*Susie Field*

## The Enormous Turnip

An old man once went planting, sowed rows of turnip seeds.
Then watched them grow through rain and shine and plucked
out ghastly weeds.
One turnip by exception had speed and grew in haste.
The old man raised excitement as he dreamed about the taste.

So soon the turnip ripened, the perfect thing for tea.
The man he gathered all his might to set the turnip free.
He pulled and nothing shifted, deep breath and strength to find.
Alas he had to call his wife and soon she stood behind.

'Heave ho,' still nothing happened, they'd need more help to win
This battle of the turnip, so a passing boy joined in.
But still their strength was lacking; a girl then joined the line.
And then a dog, a cat and mouse, so eager now to dine.

With all their might, slight movement, the turnip shifted fast
And knocked the party off their feet and oh now how they laughed.
The biggest turnip ever, all helped to bring inside.
And whilst the wife prepared the meal, they sat eyes hungry-wide.

As much as they could manage, the old man, dog and cat,
His wife, the boy, the girl, the mouse, tucked in 'til they felt fat.
With only one third eaten, the turnip paved the way,
Turnip soup and turnip pie for tomorrow and a day!

*C J Ireson*

## STRANGE BUT TRUE

It was 1990 on July 1st that we first set foot and didn't imagine
the worst
It wasn't really evident the horrors that were in store
when we stepped over the threshold and through the opened door!
Everything seemed so perfect, we really were quite proud,
It was definitely worth it, we'd tell everyone out loud
The work we'd put into our lovely new house, we'd look into the field
and occasionally spot a mouse
The setting was truly wonderful you see, we couldn't imagine what
was to be.
As time went on we became really sad, we didn't know why we were
feeling so bad
The house was now finished and looked beautiful and calm,
but somewhere, something was causing us harm
I'd always felt awkward being left alone, I felt as though there was
someone watching me in my home
My thoughts I'd keep them all to myself, I began to notice it was
affecting my health
I would tell my husband of the feelings I'd had, he didn't understand at
first, how this presence could be bad
As time went by and things got worse, we began to feel we'd
been cursed
A heavy atmosphere was in my home, friends didn't visit much and
relatives let us alone
It was plainly obvious that something was wrong, when we first
encountered that terrible pong!
The smell was vile and was getting so bad, my husband and I became
very very sad
What could we do to alleviate the smell? Air fresheners and purifiers
could not rid us of this hell
A friend suggested that we should see a priest, he came and blessed
our house with Holy water, this gave us some relief
However, soon after, the problem came right back, much worse
this time than before, it really did attack

The smell was really awful what else was there we could do?
So we contacted a medium, not one but two
The first one came and told us he'd rid our home of this, he told
the culprit to get out and this he truly did
The house began to feel better by the day, safer at night, but something
still didn't really feel quite right
So we invited another medium to take a look, when he came, he realised
that something still was stuck
Apparently we'd been visited by a soul or two, they came in through
the bathroom, a vortex near our loo
The visitor became stronger the more we began to fear, we hadn't
realised that we were drawing it near
He dealt with our problem and sent it on its way, we all said a little
prayer, we waited, what a day!
It's been a long time since we went through all of this. Looking back
things really did get bleak
The moral here is to be strong and never ever weak.

*Chris Needley*

## A NEW BEGINNING

This story begins where another one ends -
And though told in rhyme, it is one of our time.

He sat there alone, ragged and dejected on a park bench.
Why was he there? Shivering in the winter air -
Once he had been a husband and lover - the best around -
A family man - good at heart, honest and sound.

The rot set in when he met some 'friends' in a bar
They told him his talent could make him a 'star'!
They could make a 'killing', playing gigs with 'All Star' billing!
Money flowed in thick and fast - it really was too good to last.

He enjoyed the new life, and soon forget his home and wife.
On the road, day after day, at many venues they did play.
Money, drugs, sex and booze - what was there for him to lose!

'You only live once' - so 'Go with the flow'
'Don't be a fool' - 'It's good to be cool!'
'Forget the past' - 'It really wasn't meant to last' -
This is the life!

These words went around and around in his head.
Now he wished that he were dead -
The lifestyle had taken its deadly toll.

He was in a large black hole - unable to deliver!
Hence, left deserted and alone - this is no fiction -
Nursing a serious drug addiction.

It is uphill all the way from now on - no easy way out!
In order to last, he must acknowledge his past -
So he can start a new beginning!

*Mary Fitzpatrick-Jones*

## VISITING TIME

Grey heads nod in unison
  The whiff of stale urine lingers.
Millie greets you hands outstretched
  Rising unsteadily on ulcered legs
Her plea is just a hand to hold.
  Rob in cancer's grip vents his annoyance
Through withered lips.
  Elizabeth shuffles by unaware
A rapid burping from the rear.
  Derrick forever never still
Living as a business king.
  Move your legs you stupid cow
His imagined trip four days behind.
  Long-legged Ann wrapped in a shawl
'Me head's cold, oh dear me head's cold,'
  Dum de dum drones in song.
Maria's frail frame does a feeble jig
  Got to get my fat off
'I'm a naughty girl,' insists.
  Mick has had an accident, trousers very wet
Oblivious to young nurses' charm
  As helped off to comfort, change.
With manhood in permanent recoil
  Coal mine and dominoes his link to reality.
As bodies and minds recede into the past
  Soon all will be discarded
Maybe for a bright new start.
  Visiting time awakes you to the fact
The hands of time are out of grasp.

*Robert Fallon*

## BAD DAY

There are some days when it is best
To just stay in bed and take a rest
For if you venture out of the door
Only trials and tribulations galore
Are waiting, so that everything
You do, is doomed before you begin.

I should have stayed at home today
It was dreadful in a mundane way
Got out of bed and stubbed my toe
My unmatched clothes just did not go
Spilt milk and toothpaste on them too
Spent ages searching for a missing shoe.

Reassured myself whilst on my knees
That troubles only come in threes
Then the bus simply did not arrive
My boss was convinced I meant to skive
I'd walked all the way in the rain
Feet, legs and ankles were in pain.

Perhaps that's why my patience snapped
And why my good manners lapsed
As I gave him a piece of my mind
A written warning he said I'd find,
Would be in the post before too long
We both agreed I was in the wrong.

No sandwiches as the shop had sold out
So for my lunch I'd go without,
I think it's because I had not eaten
That I upset the entire meeting
They said it was just my tone
So I decided to go straight home.

*P S D MacArthur*

## MY LITTLE ANGEL

Every time I hold her
Tenderly in my arms
Look at her beautiful
Little face
And kiss her soft little
Lips
I know in my arms
I'm holding an angel
An angel of beauty
From Heaven above
An angel of beauty
I will always love
With the whole of my heart
And soul
For that angel from Heaven
Is my daughter Gemma
And she's only two years old

So thank you dear Lord above
For such a beautiful angel to love
For as long as I live on the world

*Donald John Tye*

## TILL SPRING UNTIL THEN

A flurry of fur grey
comes every single day
the visitor begs outside the doors
exquisite little face
expressive cute paws

Peanuts, custard creams
most buried whole, a favourite delight
tulips hyacinths and the daffodils upended
a sad, sorry plight.
When not in the kitchen this little scrap
knows where to scrounge, fidgets
gaining attention looking appealing
the patio by the lounge.

Beware! Danger lurks on the carpeted floor
slit-eyed black panther like cat
obsessively jealous paranoiac territorial
fangs mean fast and all that.
With matchless agility run squirrel run
trust him not, climb high the trees
for when hunting a useless command
'Come down at once! . . . Oscar . . . *Please'*

Considered a pest the squirrel
born the wrong shade, so they say
to me you are enchanting
irresistible in such a sweet way.
In the long silence of winter
when you tuck down in bed
bulbs to bloom the borders returned
and tools go back in the shed.

The silence is lonely, without you
the garden seems empty and bare
Oscar sleeps by radiators possibly in dreams
on safari, big game hunting there
*Till spring* little one, when you awake
and full of fun rise
a mid-winter glimpse before welcome - well maybe
*Until then* your image I keep in my eyes.

**Mildred F Barney**

## ISLAND OF REFUGE

Trudi was a dachshund
A sausage dog and brown
She went upon a holiday
To Littlehampton town.

The beach was good for digging
With front paws and with snout
I nose sand piled up between her legs
She kicked the whole lot out.

It showered upon her owner
A-lying in the sun
He swore and sat up smartly
'Go swimming! It's more fun!'

Now Trudi was a dachshund
A sausage dog and small
To waddle in the gentle waves
Was not her thing at all.

She waded till she floated
Then paddled with her feet
A submarine of flailing legs
The worst you'll ever meet.

She panicked as she floundered
And paddled round and round
She looked in desperation
And then an island found:

A woman in a bathing-suit
Was bending, huge and black
The dachshund stuck her claws in
And clambered on her back.

The woman spluttered forward
An angry, screaming gran
The dachshund bounded shorewards
And to her owner ran.

She panted in the sunlight
Dripped water from her jaws
Black pieces of a bathing-suit
Still clinging to her claws.

So if your dog is digging
In Littlehampton sand
Just keep your dachshund with you
For fear of where she'll land.

*Harold Wonham*

## THREATENING INTRUDER

I pulled back the covers and sat upright, fully awake and alert,
A sound had woken me, not the nightmare with its imagined hurt.

Banishing the horrors, the bad dream evoked, I got up to investigate,
Half-way down the stairs I paused, what if the noise as a clever
criminal's bait?

At this thought, panic froze my footsteps, so I sat down quietly
on a stair,
And hearing another muffled bang, I reached deep for courage upon
my sleeve to wear.

I achieve the descent, and switched lights on, my fears to dispel,
From another room a loud crash sounded ,with difficulty, I controlled
a terrible yell.

Dialling 999 was my instinct, but the commotion had come from
the room with the telephone,
I could not scream or shout, but from the back of my throat
I unsuccessfully smothered a groan.

Being alone in the middle of the night, summoning help from the
police, was my single option,
Gingerly moving toward the telephone I started shaking, what if
they had a gun?

My blood became solid in my veins as I saw something red flash past
from the corner of my eye,
In the next instant I felt I was going to faint as my blood pressure
rocketed sky high.

The terror in the pit of my stomach eased as I realised my potential
assassin's tiny size,
And in that second I learned that however warm the day, leaving doors
open is not wise.

This is how entry was attained yesterday by my uninvited guest who put my sleep pattern in a whirl,
And creeping gently closer I saw, trembling with fear in the corner was a baby red squirrel!

*Joy R Gumstone*

## FACT OR FICTION

We flew to that island of granite.
Wild, savage, that land of the Marquis.
Relief from our provincial homeland.
So, taking the first train next morning,
We saw ancient citadels rising
'Gainst backcloth of flushed early dawning.

Too soon came the time for departure.
We boarded our train, sat down gladly.
But shortly we stopped in the wilderness,
Impatiently waiting and fuming.
At last we saw something approaching,
A train somewhat dingy and dirty.

It seemed to gain speed far too quickly
Via ravines, frail bridges, steep inclines.
Through derelict stations, black tunnels.
Now battered and bruised we were falling -
One side to the other we tumbled.
Old Nick, himself, surely was driving.

We feared we were doomed to encircle
Forever that isle of the Devil.
When shuddering halt left us breathless.
Dishevelled, we fell on the platform.
Our saturnile driver leaned leering,
As slowly we limped to our hostel.

'So sorry we're late,' we all muttered.
Our host clearly thought we were tipsy.
And gave us such withering glances.
'In fact you are five minutes early,'
We gazed at each other in horror.
The truth, was it real, or just fiction?

*Biddy Redgrove*

## PLIGHT OF MARY JONES

They buried a widow just the other day
No one came, no one stayed
She raised a family
Husband Jack, died tragically
Driving drunk in his motor car
Hitting Sir John's tree on property
His life was only 33, then Mary lost her life

Pushing at Sir John's wife
You see Jack had an affair
As poor Mary fell down the stairs

*James Patrick Milton*

# RANDALLEX AND THE STONE OF LIGHT

Upon a time, upon a place,
Where glorious steeples pierced the sky, where castles stood in mists
of cloud -
A valiant knight did live there.
Sir Randallex rode with vigour and grace to lead King Herm to victory,
So doing did he win the heart of the daughter of His Majesty.
Fair Merelda once did espy a handsome warrior fleeting by;
And from that day her affects were for but one - Sir Randallex.

All was perfect, all in peace,
Until a creature blanketed the sky with blackness as it soared above
The vast dominion of King Herm. Across the land a rapid crease
Of fire wrought sorrow and despair, many perished in devouring flames
Breathed by the dragon who hungered for death to men. He of
'Many Names' was loathed by King Herm, who said, 'I'll put a price
upon his head.'
Sir Randallex did raise his sword,
Merelda quivered, 'I accept, Lord.'

She begged him no, she loved him so,
His hand she clasped in hers so tight, declared she could not
live without
Her wayfaring warrior so brave and bold. Yet Randallex spoke,
'I must go. Merelda, thou shalt take this stone and therefore crumble not
of fear.
If I live, Lihtan Stan shall shine whene'er thou holdest it near.'
And a box he placed into her hands, wherein an egg-shaped stone
shone bright:
Lihtan Stan, the Stone of Light.

One score of days, two score more,
Still Randallex voyaged through tempests strong until an isle came
into view,
A desolate cave festooned in smoke.
His ship he moored upon the shore,
His shield he arched upon his back, his helm he placed on his head;
His sword he released from its scabbard. And Randallex entered into
the black,
And Merelda shivered as she beheld
Lihtan Stan lose all its light.

*Vanessa Jackson*

## HEAVENLY IMAGE

The accident was horrendous, a lad lay in the road.
A bike, nearby on fire, almost ready to explode,
No one but me around, as he lay bleeding on the ground.
Immediately using my phone to call 999
My only hope was that the services would get there on time
How could someone just not care leaving him there to die.
As I went to comfort the lad I happily heard him sigh,
I covered him with a car blanket, so as he wouldn't get cold,
Although I never moved him I could see he wasn't that old.
Almost at once the ambulance came, but I couldn't tell them
Who was to blame, safely aboard a stretcher I could now get
On my way,
But one of the strangest things happened to me that very day,
The car refused to start, it had been no trouble for years.
By now it was trying my patience, and I was very close to tears,
I sat there for a moment my hands on the steering wheel,
Then looking through the windscreen, what I saw just couldn't be real.
A figure of a young woman stood there beckoning me
I was absolutely petrified, I know that she could see
But as she came closer, she had a kindly face
I just wished that I wasn't here, couldn't wait to leave the place.
Then she spoke, and thanked me for caring for her lad
Then her eyes filled with tears, that made me feel so sad
You see, I'm not of this Earth, but, from Heaven above
I can only look down on my son, sending him my love
But now I'll let you go on your way
And thank you again for this day.
Then she vanished out of sight
And my car seemed to start alright!

*Sheila Buckingham*

# FOOTPRINTS OF THE CHILD

She walks all day . . . everyday,
along the beaches of Acapulco,
her ragged, pink-flowered dress
bleached by summer's unrelenting sun,
no ribbons adorn her long, black hair.
Plastic sandaled shoes leave small footprints behind,
hot sugary sand soon washed away
by the sea of a thousand others following behind.
No smile illuminates this beautiful child's face
as she watches others frolic in the sea.

'Hola, hermosa dama, buy my shell bracelets?'
A child's voice softly echoes . . .
an old woman gazes from nine-year-old eyes.
'Pay for my song, pretty lady?'
'Yes, please sing your favourite song for me'
and she does . . . in Spanish.
Sad, sweet, lilting tones, hauntingly bored.
Life's lessons learned much too young.
She must earn her way . . . no child's play for her,
today or tomorrow.

'What do the words mean?'
'A man loves a woman, kills her . . . and then is sad.'
'Thank you. Here's a peso for your efforts.'
So much guilt . . . paying so little . . . for so much given.
'Gracias,' the melancholy voice whispers.
The woman-child turns, towards her future . . .
lessons of enduring fortitude learned under each umbrella,
following, being followed by generations of
proud, honest, hardworking people
reflecting the fundamental strength of Mexico.

***Polly Davies***

# REJECTION

What can we do when life turns sour
When hateful words
Like knives of steel
Burn through the flesh
Into our soul
Destroys the love,
The peace, the calm
Of all that went before

The years of growth
When all was well
When children sang
And hearth and home
Meant happiness for all
For evermore.

What does it take
To heal the pain
Of sleepless nights
That merge and fall
To days of sorrow
Grief and tears.

It takes the greatest effort known,
To rise above the murk and mire
The shattered dreams,
The hopes and plans,
That we have nurtured
Through the years.

As time goes by
The lessons learned
Will surely bring us hope anew
That peace and goodness can prevail
And joy and love
Return to you.

**Pat Plant**

## INNOCENCE LOST

It was a story about when she was five
She was taught a lesson on how to survive
He wasn't supposed to touch her like that
But he did and there's no turning back

It wasn't something she was gonna forget
But it was something Uncle would regret
Looked in a cell for the rest of his life
Leaving a son behind and a sorry wife

It wasn't something that I should hear
Too much for my tender years
Such a shock I couldn't have known
Things were kept secret long ago

I wonder how many women there is
Who've had their lives f***** up like this?
Keeping quiet 'cause of the shame
Just who are they really trying to save?

When you're a child you don't know
You take what they give then let you go
It's true some get caught for the abuse
Some they never catch or turn loose

And on with your life try to forget
Innocence lost shouldn't know about that just yet
But it's always in the back of the mind
And you can't rust men for a very long time

Never again will you turn your back
When you're taken down an old dirty track
What he's after you really know
It's yours to give only if you feel it so

*David McDonald*

# WHEN THE BOATS CAME IN

Time was when trawlers lined the beach at Beer
Chugging off at daybreak, boats full of fishing gear.
Manned by rugged Devon men, bearded, tanned and weathered,
Out at sea they trawled their nets, the pots were laid and tethered.
Eyes so blue from constant searching for signs of wind and rain,
Or waves so great, a timely warning to return to land again.

Against the elements they toiled all day.
Eventide homecoming watched across the bay.
Then as each boat prepared for beaching,
Circling seagulls, squawking, screeching,
Eager helpers, young and old,
Made for a place on the capstan pole.
The catch unloaded, plaice, mackerel, huss red mullet
Sold and gutted, offal snatched down seagulls' gullet.
The groups dispersed, the men went home.
Nostalgic memories these scenes can capture
But now technology, devoid of rapture,

Ensures a switch will take the place of willing hands and eager face.
Though that was many years ago and changes there have been,
Still the shelters on the cliff and the rail on which to lean,
To gaze at sea and chalky cliffs peculiar to Beer alone,
For up and down the coast from there is mostly red sandstone.
The fishing boats still go to sea, though these days they are fewer,
But there is yet so much to keep the interest of the viewer.
The village nestling in the valley, and though larger than of yore
Maintains its charm, individuality
And ever calls me home.

*Jean W Sumelka*

## DON'T DRINK

It was her boyfriend's birthday.
He said, 'Let's go to the village pub,
One drink won't hurt, what about two?'
'Be careful,' she said, 'you almost hit that car.'
He laughed, 'You sound more and more like your ma.'
The rugby team were at the pub shouting,
'We've won! We've won! Drinks for everyone '
'One drink won't hurt, what about two?'
A young man rushed in.
'My wife's just had twins, drinks all round.'
'One drink won't hurt, what about two?'
Two pretty girls put their arms around him.
'We've just passed our tests, will you have a drink with us?'
'One drink won't hurt, what about two?'
His girlfriend walked over to his side.
'Please don't drink and drive.'
He pushed her away.
'Are you trying to spoil my fun?'
An old man in the corner said,
'You should listen to her son.'
The barman said,
'You've had enough, it's time for you to go.'
Her boyfriend staggered to the door.
'Now where did I park the car?'
'There's another pub in this village.
One drink won't hurt, what about two?'
He was swerving everywhere.
'Too many trees around here,' he said as he changed gear.
Lights off other cars drew near.
She screamed. Everything went black.
At his funeral she heard someone say,
'There's a pub in the village, one drink won't hurt, what about two?'

*Sandra Wood*

# THE LITTLE BLUE JUG

'Choose me,' said the jug in the corner
In a corner where no daylight shone
Just a rattle of pots for a second
And the hope - for that moment - had gone
He'd sat in a corner forever so long
Sometimes he wondered if it were something he'd done.
He came from a factory quite near Stoke-on-Trent
Where he'd been painted a beautiful blue
With a fine golden line at the edge at the top
And a gold line round the bottom edge too.
Last time he was out he was filled with mint sauce
A cube of sugar to sweeten as well,
Cider vinegar, chopped mint leaves of course,
But he wasn't too keen on the smell!
One day his lady was given some flowers
A most beautiful bunch of sweet peas
Delicately perfumed, mauve, red and pink
She thought: *I know what would be perfect for these.*
Her hand reached right into his corner
And she lifted him down from the shelf
She washed him and dried him and polished him up
Oh! He was so proud of himself!
Now he stands in a prominent place in the hall
Where even the postman can see
And he smiles at himself in the mirror
And he thinks - *now* -
*Everyone's looking at me!*

*Pam S Quigley*

## TRAIL

Cycled into Burnley
at sorting office posted off new story
popped into Sainsbury's
to do top up bit of shopping.
Met Philippa collecting her bike from Halford's
peddling together back along the canal
festooned with ducks, drakes and ducklings,
new life along the way
sheltered by nettles overhanging from the banks
a flotilla of energy
protected by a stinging jungle.

Lunching later at Barden Mill
still beside the canal
watching and being watched by
various ages of ducklings
in the early summer sunlight
following their parents
feathering the trail.

*Robert D Shooter*

## PHANTOM

Downstream majestic he drifted
Graceful, head drooping in sadness
Eyes shut in utter rejection

Anguish, a total despairing
Grief overwhelming, heartbreaking
Loneliness, why did it happen?

Then by his side such pure beauty
Elegant, long neck extended
Shocked, he was not comprehending

Was it? It couldn't be, could it?
Did all that cruelty happen
Wondering - Oh! how he loved her

Drifting downstream back together
While his heart sang, such great sadness
She disappeared. Just a phantom

Downstream majestic he drifted
Graceful, head drooping in sadness
Eyes shut in utter dejection

*Enid Gill*

## WHO'D HAVE THOUGHT IT?

I only went to buy a ribbon for my word processor, cost would be about
five pounds, but it cost a whole lot more,
Seventy to be exact, no I kid you not, for never in your wildest dreams,
would you guess what I have got,
For ages I have plodded on, happy and content, not wanting very much
from life, not caring where I went,
But all that is about to change, on that each one can bet, for I have
joined up, yes I have, on the Internet.

A shock to all I must admit, especially to me, me upon the Internet,
I never thought I'd see,
And yet I'm here and here I'll stay, until I'm word perfect, unless
I throw it through the door, or cut away its net,
That's not to say I will not try, I'll give it all I've got, that's if I last
more than a day, at the moment I think not,
The mouse keeps going off the page, these squares keep jumping out,
I'm sure I've seen a little man, from the back come running out.

I've read my windows dumber book, from front right to the back,
I can quote it word for word, it's the knowledge that I lack,
My fingers won't do as they're told, my brain keeps closing down,
in fact I should have stayed at home, and not gone into town,
I now know how to turn it on, and turn it off again, I'm getting quite
excited,
well I am, not my brain,
That's still running round in circles, blowing bubbles, singing songs,
I think I'll switch it off again, I can't do that job wrong.

The steam is coming out my ears, my language is profound, I've met
myself at least three times, going round and round,
Yet I can see some changes now, things are slowly sinking in, I can now
see the future, and also where I've been,
It's taken most of all the day, into the evening time, but if you ask me
now, I'll say it's coming on quite fine,
The machine is still in one piece, my face is not as flushed, my hair is
sitting in its place, and I'm not out of puff.

From shouting at the screen or even turning off and on, believe me if you called today, it wouldn't be much fun,
You would not have been spoken to, nor let inside the door, for I was much too busy having tantrums on the floor,
They say it takes a while to be an expert at this task, that could mean years to me, if you pass my house just pass,
Yet I am one day wiser, but tomorrow I'll forget, all I've learned myself today, on this stupid Internet.

*Kathleen Townsley*

## BADGE MCKENNA'S GOLD

There was a kettle full a'cider on that mongrel's cookin' stove
and a fly-blown egg in a swillin' cup, a few reckin' weeks old,
a quarter horse that stuck its head inside the cabin door and
two mules out the back with dirty saddle sores.
His name was Badge McKenna, cos he used ta' be a sheriff,
'til he kicked a man to death inside his cell.
Then he made a run like thunder, found a hideout in the mountains
with a bounty of reward upon his tail.
He was big an' round an' swollen with green bruises on his knuckles,
from stranglin' every creature he could find,
wore skunk skin on his head and rabbit feet for buckles,
hung carcasses along a fishin' line.
Each day he'd track the river with a flat pan and a shovel,
seekin' him the gold of what he'd heard, as quiet as a tiger,
siftin' sneaky as a shiver, swillin' for his riches in the dirt.
Come winter he was desperate, when the snow was heavy driven
and not a single sliver had he found.
He was meaner than a jackal snared upon a thicket,
gettin' leaner every day by the pound.
The mules was lame with foot rot and the quarter horse had bolted
and everythin' around him seemed ta' ail,
he bound his feet with beaver, rigged some shoes up with a slipknot
and took him to the river with his pails.
And in the dead a' nightfall with the kerosene an' moonlight
he grappled him a twinkle from the bed, cracked it with his teeth,
damn near broke his slimy molars
and roared a cackle fit ta' wake the dead.
He'd hit himself a fortune, no bigger than a fanny,
but deeper than a fanny with no shame - it would see ta' his undoin'
for there were other eyes a plenty, bounty hunters eyein' up his claim.

He didn't hear the danger, didn't feel the bullets,
as the Murphy brothers riddled him with lead,
he only saw the yeller in the colour a' the nugget
as he belched his final stinkin' lung a' breath.
And that there seam became a legend as the golden tale got twisted,
but never a more wealthy story told, and lyin' neath the river,
with cold water for a blanket, is Badge McKenna, buried with his gold.

*Maria Daines*

# A SAD END

The office party was over, Shelley picked up her things from the
luxury flat she lived in, 'Christmas presents for the family', and left,
eager to get away down the motorway in her Porsche,
to be together again with her family for Christmas.

Shelley saw her parents only once a year and loved the luxury of
her parents and their home, and being waited on by her mother
who loved to have her there.

The drive was stressful, but now off the motorway, she could relax
a little. Soon she turned into a leafy driveway
and made her way slowly along, humming to herself happily,
as she arrived at the front door there was her mother waiting
with open arms, 'joined by her father', she parked up
and walked across to the door when she was hugged to death.

Shelley felt like the luckiest girl in the world.
A log fire burned away in the hearth.
There was a huge Christmas tree in the corner of the room sparkling
with trimmings, underneath were parcels piled high.
She looked through the French window onto a large garden,
It had started to snow and the flakes came down like cotton wool
floating in the air.

Shelley went into the kitchen where a wonderful smell came from
and opened the oven door to see a huge golden turkey,
stuffing, and roast potatoes, and 'lots more'.

She went for a hot bath in the luxury bathroom, and was greeted by
her mother, when she came down with a glass of sherry and a mince
pie.
For a while she sat in the armchair by the fire
watching the snowflakes falling through the window.

Shelley woke up to the door bell ringing and laughter
and in walked Grandma and Uncle Frank followed by some neighbours
who had called to say Merry Christmas.
She noticed that her father was not around,
her mother said he had gone for a walk.

Everyone who mattered was there and they sat around the table
for Christmas Eve dinner,
Shelley saw that her mother looked tearful and wasn't herself,
and where was Dad? Then her mother burst into tears,
'I'm sorry,' she said, 'I wanted to wait until Christmas was over before
I told you, but I can't hide how I feel any longer,' she turned to Shelley.
'I am sorry darling there won't be another Christmas like this.'

Shelley was stunned that this secure place, or the place she was so sure
of was to be sold, her parents could not afford to live there any more
and must move somewhere else, things would never be the same again.

*Jean Bailey*

## UNTITLED

High-up on hickory, I see the world -
The world is square.

My whiskers quiver, my heart beats below my fur,
But I am no longer aware of my small body.
For I see the world, so far down there -
The world is square.

Our universe is a cube in which
Strange objects float above our flat square world.
The sun dangles by a thread.

Tick-tock, tick-tock, my rocket begins to shudder,
I fear the atmosphere up here may be breaking it apart -
*Dong!* A tremendous crash, the rocket vibrates wildly,
And I ran down.

*Paula Holt*

# IN AGE

In age they say, is wisdom gold'n - virtue's own particular currency
in excess of shiny bullion . . .

In age shall our fairest beauty wane
In age therefore shall we much disdain;
In age our sharpest grief shall manifest
In age slight regard breeds bitter loneliness;
In age o'er quick youth greets slow demise
In age all temperate counsel lies;
In age shall we shrink and sigh
In age shall we fear all and cry
In age shall we think to die
In age we'll sit alone and ponder why;
In age shall we become most odd
In age shall we earnestly court the favour of our god;

In age therefore, are we thus transform'd, though our greying locks
shalt
court much scorn. Yet, before our wisdom let youth's arrogance
stand thus redress'd, for in our shoes are they yet doomed to step.

*M Dixon*

# THIS GREEN AND PLEASANT LAND

A tiny inn of cobbled stone nestles snugly in a vale
The rock extruded into life, to compliment a mulling ale.
A crackling fire of oaken logs, sends smoke into a breezeless spire,
And patrons gently stir the world, whilst stoking up a patient briar.

The ancient, straining, blackened beams encrusted with their
limpet brass,
Stare down on carefully polished flags, retaining strength for time
to pass.
Conversations centuries old absorbed into their very grain.
When men once sat in powdered wigs, with booty from
the Spanish main.

Only they remember days, when they were cut so firm and stout.
Holding planking, decking, rigging. Men within and seas without.
Until the night that nature challenged, storms too violent off the Cape,
The wind went howling, men died screaming, keel and ribs
the washed up shape.

A hundred years it lay and weathered, seasoned oak of fifty tons,
Then dragged and cut to fit the rock, by sons of sailors sons or sons.
As though in final retribution, cleaved and hacked to sail no more,
It sits as doomed to hold the roof, from travellers passing
through the door.

September time. The hand of autumn, paints the leaves a burnished
gold.
Time for trees to quietly snooze, awaiting winter's icy cold.
Nature with her choice of season, keeps the treadmill of mankind,
Ever turning, always testing. Weeding out the weak of mind.

Coddled comfort, selfish Man, has taken all replacing none,
Genetic blindness to his peril, likened to the Lemmings' run.
Intelligent in all he touches, nature twisted out of tune.
'Let us alter all the seasons, burn the forests shoot the moon!'

Gone the days of quiet living, animals all bred to die,
Have no say in their existence; can pigs walk or chickens fly?
fishmeal fed for three short months, piglets fattening for the roast.
Egg machines in living Hell, laying breakfasts, pass the toast!

Brontosaurus served his purpose, Men evolved to take his place,
Now his body fires our engines, taking us through time and space.
Will Men be important too - the generations left behind?
A flooded Earth, no trees for shade, a scalding sun to sear the mind.

His epitaph reads 'Rape and Pillage, Flora/Fauna dying here,'
Reaping more than he can sow, his own extinction very near.
What a caring, sharing world? The Son of God disbelieves.
'Was this what I suffered for, crucified between the thieves?'

'Time to halt this march of 'progress'. Time to bring man
down to Earth.'
'Time to show him who decides and shrink his head of swollen girth.'
'A tiny Inn should serve the purpose, one with history so divine;
That I can show how insecure, a man can be within this shrine.'

'With every ounce of Co2, with every sacrificial tree,
I'll count as atoms in a nail, until there is enough for Three!'
'Then as Calvary Man will find, that he was made to be as me,
Not to rape this world I gave him, not to be the Pharisee.'

'For I was born within a stable, just outside this very door,
So I return to my beginnings, must I save Mankind once more?'
'But first I'll alter all his values, no gold, nor frankincense and myrrh,
Mammals, trees and air are priceless, educating Man to share.

Making rarities abundant, they'll lose value overnight.
Stripping greedy men of chattels, 'til they finally see the light.
Mankind will learn humility, learn how nature operates.
Learn that all his gold is worthless, if he finally *suffocates.*'

*Andrew V Ascoli*

## CANON LAW

Henry Brown sat daydreaming at his desk
in the tiny office just inside the cathedral.
He was quiet, middle-aged, balding and
unremarkable in every way.

He came to with a start at the sound of swearing,
boys' loud voices and the desperate please of a
young woman teacher: 'Daryl Smith put that
firework down *please.*'
'Make me,' sneered a trendy ten-year-old
making ready to hurl it into the entrance
of the cathedral and egged on by his followers.

Henry leapt to his feet, snatched up the Bishop's
cassock and mitre which were waiting to be sent
to the cleaners, and put them on. Then he strode
to the top of the steps and stood with his arms
stretched wide. He looked out at a group of
unruly children running rings around the teacher.

Henry drew himself up and in a loud and terrible
voice shouted, 'Daryl Smith bring that firework to
me *now* - God is watching you. The rest of you
get in line and be quiet and respectful before you
enter God's house.'

There was instant silence as a shocked and
shame-faced Daryl did as he was told watched by
the rest. Then they all quietly filed in.

The Magistrate studied Henry and said, 'Mr Brown
I admire your desire to protect the cathedral from
vandalism nevertheless you did break the law by
impersonating the Bishop. I sentence you to
50 hours Community Service. Perhaps they're
looking for a caretaker up at the school.'

*Betty Nevell*

# I WAS THERE

To be there is a dream come true,
eighty thousand voices and a sky of blue.
Hên Wlad Fy Nhadau, booms out loud,
if Mam was here, she would be so proud.

I've seen the Haka, they look really mean,
red and black on a baize of green.
The whistle's gone; I'm going to give my all,
then I get my hands on the oval ball.

Side-stepping, dummying my way to the line,
my lungs are bursting, I get there in time.
The stadium erupts; I'm everyone's hero,
Wales seven points, New Zealand zero.

The battle goes on; it's anyone's game,
to lose this now would be a crying shame.
The forwards tackle without a minute's rest,
it's a massive effort, against the world's best.

The black sea erupts; they are on a roll,
they've taken the lead, and it's taking its toll.
The crowd demands more, they are craving a win,
Calon Lân and Delilah can be heard in the din.

Full time is looming, we have to attack,
find a way through a thick line of black.
A moment of genius, a chip ahead,
the stadium erupts, in a sea of red.

A race to the line, we've scored at the death,
a conversion to win, we all hold our breath.
The silence is deafening, not even a cough,
oh no it can't be, my alarm's just gone off!

***Percy Jones***

# THE NIT NURSE

The Nit Nurse she was coming upon her burdened bike
A buxom woman size unknown she was a jolly sight
She was a fixture on the roads where workmen feigned a wink
At bloomers strangling both her knees . . . usually blue or pink

Her bike was rammed into a ramp where tyres breathed a sigh
Lightened they of all her weight, theirs not to reason why
We kids all smirked, those knickers as she bent to grab her pump
And gambled if the dress would split in protest of her rump

For we all knew the truth of it she'd come to hunt for nits
And woe betide the child found out she'd scour that head to bits
And if she found a reprobate she'd yank the darn thing out
Happy with her hunting day . . . 'Eureka,' she would shout

We lads would form a line to left the girls would queue the right
Wondering on the poor fool found whose shame would come to light
You prayed you would not be the cause of Archimedean joy
As expert hands did ruffle heads of every girl and boy

They'd die a death these lodgers their dash for freedom squashed
Carbolic soap would bomb the scalp till every hair was washed
When satisfied all heads were well she'd leave for pastures new
With bloomers once again on show . . . usually pink or blue

*M J Banasko*

## IVAR BEINLAUS

They married but the prophesy stated
an immediate consummation would be ill-fated.
Ragner should wait for three clear days,
but being fiery in his ways
took his wife straight to bed
risking a future birth would upon them dread.

There seems to be a mystery
as to their offspring's history.
Born under the shadow of a spell
foretelling the child would be unwell,
was Ivar a deformed child
or a nine foot giant who was wild!

Ivar Beinlaus as he was named
a warrior Viking believed untamed.
Beinlaus or Boneless to us
so form this name we only guess,
that agility with double joints
feasible from which our knowledge points,
but brittle bones seems far from fact
as he produced as a normal act.

Twelve hundred years ago
a child deformed and weak in stature,
would have been killed from what we know
of Vikings, as even their kind didn't matter.
Ivan Beinlaus was nine foot tall,
a warrior giant no one could fall.

*David Thomas*

# SO IT BEGINS . . . SO IT MUST END

1945 - The world's at peace, for now. Conflict over and done.
A young boy's just begun . . . Jarvis & Son, IFE M & C.
The gate man glares at George Dunn.
'Main office, over there, knock and wait.'
Tender white knuckles against a solid oak door. A voice booms loud.
'Who the friggin' 'ell's that knockin' this time o' the morning?'
'George Dunn Sir,' is the mumbled, trembling reply.
The voice from within booms yet again. 'Get your arse to the fitting
shop double quick . . . find Terry Stokes . . . that's Mr to you sunshine.'
The boy turns and walks away, into a world of smoke, fire and steam.
Every inch of ground vibrates from the constant hammering
and banging.
Furnaces full to the brim . . . white hot boiling metal. Fresh air . . . nah!
A million sparks cascade down upon old men of thirty.
Covered in muck and grime, soaked in sweat.
They stare, but not at the boy . . .
One of the metal monsters is about to disgorge its insides of molten
metal. It tips slowly at first, then faster . . . into the floor channels.
Watch out boy . . . I bite.

1965 - Two decades . . . been and gone. George has down well,
No 2 to Terry Stokes. Jarvis & Son, IFE, no longer M & C,
have not fared as well.

1985 - He's reached the last furlong. Forget the yuppies,
they're not wanted here.

1995 - I wish there had been more time and space. End of the line.
Jarvis is barely an 'E' now. Most of the yard is derelict.
Old George walks across the yard for the last time.
Nothing but rusting metal . . . furnaces, steam hammers all so silent.
Does anyone want to know . . . does anyone care . . .

A leathery, well-worked hand pushes open a smoked glass door.
The cool of the air conditioning beckons.
Congratulations . . . happy birthday too. There's a cake,
in the shape of a fitting shop.
'Go on George . . . one quick blow and they'll all be blown out.
Blown away . . . just like life.'

*G J Cayzer*

## DARIUS THE DRAGON

'Darius' the dragon
Felt a kind of fake
For no matter just how hard he tried
No fire could he make

He'd clasp his scaly fingers
Across his scaly tum
And snorted very loudly
Until he woke his mum

'You cannot run before you walk,'
His mother said to him.
'First you have to make a spark
Right from down within.'

His mother now showed him how
To make the embers burn
He'd never get the hang of this
There was so much to learn

'Just relax - and take a breath
And do what I've just done . . .
Once you learn to make a spark
Your life will be more fun.'

All night the little dragon
Toiled without a break
He had to show his mamma
The fire he would make

Then suddenly a puff of smoke
Came from within his nose
This had come as some surprise -
As he'd began to doze!

He tried again and sure as not
There was a kind of fog
He kept on going until he was hoarse
His cave was full of smog!

Then there was this burning smell
Amongst his bed of leaves
Instead of being quite concerned
He felt deep down real pleased

And as the flames grew higher
He fanned them with his tail
Whilst Mum and Dad ran around
Looking for a pail

Then slosh they threw the water
Through the entrance of the cave
And shouted, 'Darius - are you still there?
Come out and you'll be saved.'

But Darius was busy looking
For a loaf of bread
He was flaming bits of toast
For his breakfast now instead

And as he piled them on a plate
His mum and dad did laugh
Said, 'Come on son - enough of this
You're off to have a bath!'

And as the flames they peter out
Doused by water from a flagon
He knew he was like the others now . . .
A fire-eating dragon!

**Anne E Roberts**

## SCHOOL DINNERS

Do you hate school dinners? I did when I was young!
They used to feed us frogs, rabbits and stewed pig tongue.

It was always horrible stuff, that we kids got to eat.
And most of the dinners, smelled like sweaty feet.

One day it was really bad, and my friend sitting next to me
Found a crunchy beetle, in her mushy peas.

She was just about to swallow it, but she spat it on the floor.
And then she pucked right up, all over the canteen door.

It ran down the door, and all around the handle.
It looked like sticky wax, dripping from a candle.

All the kids were staring, and they were all saying *yuk!*
Over came the dinner lady, she wanted to have a look.

When she saw the mess, and the sick all up the door.
Her eyes opened wide, and her chin dropped to the floor.

'What has happened here and who has just been sick?
We need to get it cleaned up, and cleaned up pretty quick.'

Then my friend said, 'There was a beetle in my lunch
and when I went to swallow, I felt a massive crunch.'

Now the dinner lady was smiling, with a big old cheesy grin.
'Oh yes I wondered, whose dinner he was in.'

'It was only our friend Bertie, but there's plenty more,
there are always loads of beetles, on the kitchen floor!'

'We won't charge you extra, for poor old little Bertie,
but next time don't be sick, don't you know it's rather dirty.'

My friend was fine, but she never ate dinners again
and she can't eat mushy peas, they'll never be the same.

I think dinners are better now, much better than they were before.
But you'll know what's happened, if you see sick up the canteen door.

***Karon Crocombe***

## THE JOURNEY

Deep in the hills,
Hidden from view,
A stream bubbles up,
Sparkling, clean and new.
Fresh from the earth,
From the womb within,
It reaches the air,
Full of vigour and vim.
Finding a way,
Through the heather and grass,
Passing unnoticed,
By rocks and ferns.
Creeping round tussocks,
And tree roots buried deep,
Downwards from the hills,
To fields full of sheep.
The journey begins,
For the stream birthed new,
Twisting and turning,
Fresh and clear of hue.
Past the shepherd boy,
Tending his flock,
For him also,
The future is locked.
His journey too,
Has just begun,
Unknown to him,
Life's twists and turns.

Where will it end?
Only God knows,
His dreams wander,
After a bubbling stream,
Down the hillside,
Beyond his sight,
Gurgling onwards,
Streaming into the night.

*Andrew P McIntyre*

## FRESH AIR

My friend next door, has a lovely crop of hair
He often makes me feel jealous, but I don't care
My hair just grows around the back and sides
Hardly any on top, it's a skating rink for flies
His wife, he tells me, tends his hair with a good shampoo
Then dries it carefully, as one should do
Chatting across the garden fence, one fine day
A gust of wind, blew the hair from his head away
He ran to pick it up, now laying on the ground
I noticed then, he had no hair, upon his crown
He replaced it quickly on his head, his face turning red
The crease in his hair, went from ear to ear, instead
I know from fact, it should have been in the middle
Hiding my face, I really had a good giggle
My hair at least is my own, I can honestly say
But the wig he wears is a sham, on show every day
I often think, as I sit in the hairdresser's chair
I never see him, I suppose the reason is, he has no hair

*W J C*

## OF MYTHS

Silver grey waters graced stone frozen,
holding our gaze and gave short sharp breaths,
tempering pounding red, red blood.
Whilst a frigid finger of fear stroked,
through quaking bodies shrouded in their clammy skins.
Warrior knights now insipid and without soul sat tremulous.
Lances idle unburdened except for the batttle's lonely ghosts.
Corpulent battle colours, vigorous fought for,
hung limp, languid and lost like,
the vague shore ahead snug baby wrapped,
in the enticing swallowing opalescent mists.
Timeless oaks clothed in emerald green swept nervously
down to first kiss the lake's surface.
Minds recoiled, urging to spy, to hope and inspire,
yet the lake from shallow to deep,
protected by a mother's arms and love.

In the reality beyond a threading glimpse of night,
clear and guiding sending eyes upward and lifting hearts
like a swallow's flight. Proud and still lies their quest.
Spirits flighted and dancing now, fixedly grazing through the
radiance falling onto their beloved Tor.

*Neal Moss*

# A NEW YORK MINUTE

Shadowed streets
A sunny day
Where did it go
Fall crisp scents
A flying show
No cares, no eyes
Only vows and hatred
What of the people
Amidst the clouds
Clinging to thoughts of work and paper
Perhaps a smile, a frown, a worry
Thinking of those not here
Then no blue sky, miles of grey
Dust
What of the people
Hopeless, almost heightless
All taken away
Indian summer, coffee and future
Smiles and happy hours, unborn children
Unmade memories and train rides
No more shadows
Only strange open space
Once filled with concrete and steel,
Dreams and life
Now empty
What of the people?

*Kate Daley*

# SILENT SERENADE

Like a noteless song, it rhymes with ease,
A silent picture to tempt and please.
A wordless melody hums its tune;
Denotes a place before we presume

Deep hues glistening
Birds are listening.

Perfectly in opposition
Faultless by composition.

Firelight dancing
Echoes chancing.

Shadows pounding
Pages sounding.

My weary eyes do finish their look
And keep a mark upon open book.
The 'morrow awaits until the dawn,
Again I'll read until twilight's born.

### *Pauline Pickin*

## THE LEGEND OF ROBOTORIA

Upon this world in centuries long past,
  Dwelt in woodland glades and pastures fresh,
The spirit of Utopia was cast
  By nymphs and faeries in their pristine flesh.

In innocence and truly wondrous way,
  Phantasms of delight would greet the dawn,
And gentle creatures thrived in ancient days,
  The phoenix and the lamb and unicorn.

Yet tides would turn and slowly parasitic
  Denizens of darkness trod the land,
With sterile minds, their trespass scientific,
  Indoctrinating methods came to hand.

Cities sprang on barely distant plain,
  Structures towered, spires of steel and glass,
Spreading like a cancer-ridden stain,
  Eating each and every blade of grass.

Streets reflected harsh magnesium glare,
  Pesticides produced with no delay,
The blackness of a future painted there
  With creeping scents of graveyards and decay.

Concrete drowned Utopia to death
  And dragged the dreams of legend down as well,
Mother Nature's lungs were starved of breath,
  False paradise defined a living Hell.

Yet gadgetry malfunctions to a halt
  And science on its own cannot set free,
The heart and soul of man by some default,
  It never is enough nor will it be.

Soon nothing moves, a chill breeze starts to blow,
  Then things that once were great or so was said,
Are drenched in sheets of radioactive snow,
  A mortuary world slabbed cold and dead.

What science could have rescued them from this?
  What reason of the night seek to undo?
For when one looks into the dark abyss,
  The dark abyss looks also into you.

Thus now the graveyard world collapses on,
  With screams engulfed in falsified euphoria,
With hopes and dreams redundant, dead and gone,
  Comes darkness, death, decay to Robotoria.

*Tony Bush*

# SIBLINGS

A little girl, under a table,
Hidden from anyone's view,
By a cloth, reaching to the floor,
So no one ever knew!
Her mother was acting strangely,
As most of the time, she did,
Not knowing what was wrong,
The child was afraid - and hid!
Her mother was alcoholic,
Loving, when she was sober,
But changed, after a glass of wine,
Terrifying - to the girl and her brother!
They only knew, when she drank wine
Suddenly she changed!
From being a loving kind of mum,
She became as a 'witch' quite deranged!
They came from school for dinner,
Nothing would be on a plate!
After cleaning the house, back to school,
In trouble, for being late!
Kind neighbours, sometimes fed them!
The sibling bond, grew strong,
War came - her brother went to fight,
He was not to be there for long.
Nineteen years old, killed in France,
His sister was broken hearted,
For sixty years, she has grieved for him,
He was her strength, until they were parted.

*E M Eagle*

# THE EX-WIFE'S TALE

*(An excerpt from 'The Wycombe Cave Tales')*

My husband you know was a pianist
And late he'd come home with Mozart and Liszt;
And though, it was said, the best in the land
His organ was neither upright nor grand!
At eighteen we wed, his hair golden thatch -
I felt truly blessed, he was quite a catch -
A long flowing mane from each tip to root;
But by twenty-five, as bald as a coot!
It was about then I had an affair -
I looked for a man with money and hair.
I met up with Dave, who asked me to stay
But in the morning, I found his toupee.
Then Malcolm and Bill, and Robert and Ben -
There must have been more, I once counted ten.
My husband found out, and so we divorced
The house, Merc and dog all his, but what's worse
They all say I'm cheap, and nought but a tart
A name ill-deserved, it does break my heart;
And now I regret the flings that I had,
I feel so alone, and endlessly sad;
But soon, I am sure, in need of a wife
A new man will come, to ruin his life.
There is no real point to this my sad tale,
Except watch your wife, if young, bald and male.

*Alex L Jones*

# EVERY POEM TELLS A STORY

Which is what I'm going to do,
The princess was walking down the lane,
And in her side she had great pain,
She met an old lady,
Who was carrying a baby,
And asked her for some help,
The old lady made the princess yelp,
As she touched the sore side,
The old lady took the princess home,
As she lived in a house with a dome,
There she gave the princess an apple to eat,
As she said that the princess shouldn't eat too much meat,
The apple made the princess feel funny,
And she fainted and had a dream about a fluffy bunny,
When the princess woke up from sleep,
There she saw seven dwarfs asleep,
And a prince going to kiss her,
She grabbed the phone and hit him,
And asked the prince what he was doing,
He told the princess after he had stopped booing,
That they were supposed to live happy ever after . . . oops.

*Catrina Lawrence*

## OUR VILLAGE POND

According to folklore, as tourists are told,
Our pond dates back to the days of old,
When the village once had a local Squire
Who had been saved from a terrible fire.

A roll of honour, the list of names
Of those who bravely fought the flames
Is carved in stone and set in the wall
Beside the entrance to our village hall

During The Great Storm, lightning struck
And as if damned by yet more bad luck,
Set ablaze the Squire's roofing thatch,
For which our fire-fighters were no match.

They ran all the way to the nearest farm
Gathered helpers and raised the alarm
They manned a chain of buckets and pails
Hurling pond water into the teeth of the gales

Amid the roar of wind and flame, a cry for help.
Thank God they'd heard this muffled yelp.
No thought for their safety, broke open a door
And rescued the Squire, found flat on the floor

Words could not express his great relief,
Glowing with generosity beyond belief,
'The pond saved me, I'll pay for its enlargement.
It shall be the best, a place of enchantment!'

So, dear visitor, when yellow flag irises gently wave,
Remember, there may be other folk yet to save.
Thus our pond, with its ferny fronds, stands resolute,
With its ranked green swords held up, in salute

***Derek Harvey***

# FREDDIE'S FEET

Hi, my name is Freddie, a Doberman by make
My colours are a black and tan; my tail's a stumpy snake
My temperament is placid, not fierce as some make out
Don't judge me by my looks alone, I'm just a pussy cat
My feet have broken out in scabs, so to the vets we trot
Mum gets some cream to rub on them, my feet are jolly hot
To alleviate the fire that is raging through my toes
I lick and lick my sticky feet, and get a runny nose!
My mum don't like me doing this, because she makes a fuss
So more cream goes upon my toes, plus some spraying stuff
Again, I lick my scabby bits; it makes them feel so good
To get my tongue between my toes, just like I knew I could
It itches so and licking helps, although it makes them red
But Mum just shouts and stamps her feet and sends me to my bed
Here comes the cream and spraying stuff,
But what's this 'yellow paste'?
It's tangy and it smells a bit - a hot and bitter taste
She's shouting at me, once again, and calling me some names
I'm not supposed to like the stuff, it's just a crying shame
So what, if I have tastebuds that like the yellow paste
She calling me a 'hot dog' now, because I like the taste
But what's this now, she's looking sad, I wonder what she's got
It's white and round and rather big - it's called a 'flower pot'
Now she's put it on my head and tied it round my neck
Am I a fashion icon now? Or rehearsing for Star Trek?
Oh, woe is me; I cannot see my tail, my feet, my 'bits'
It's held on tight for all the night, I'll have to use my wits
I have to get my head outside this stupid fashion hat
If I look sad, and all forlorn, perhaps she'll take it back?
A week has gone, my feet are fixed, no longer do they itch
They're feeling how they used to feel, (perhaps my mum's a witch).

*Sue Elle*

## UNSCHEDULED FLIGHT

If he could fly as a bird on the wing he'd soar to heights unseen,
and in his lofty silent place extol his heady pleasured dream.
Up there alone, untroubled and free and gliding in effortless style,
unencumbered by life's imperfections, he's surely linger awhile.

He would dive, and freefall, to ascend again in nonchalant tone,
and the birds-eye view from infinite space would be his and his alone.
The freedom gained would surpass all before,
his mind as clear as a bell,
the billowing breeze o'er vista serene,
would enhance the story to tell.

On flight path clear, no plan to obey, clouds all adrift on parallel road,
he'd discard the yoke of memories ache and limbs disobedient mode.
The heat of the sun and blue of the sky would impart a message dear,
and his thrill at the plunge in this headlong swoop,
dispel all hint of fear.

He thought if mankind could only join, this awesome escape in flight,
that Earth's rotation on axis fast,
would see might succumb to what's right.
He'd exhort all below to their soaring aloft
and to visions of rapture pure,
so that uplifted man could view Earth's sham
in light of Heaven's allure.

*William A Mack*

## ONCE AN ANGEL VISITED ME

Once an angel visited me
She wasn't just from a Christmas tree.
She was real and whole and before my eyes,
She said, 'Don't worry this is no surprise.
I have been with you since your life began,
To shelter you and hold your hand,
To give you strength, comfort and support,
To help you learn when you are taught.
I'm here whenever you need me
Open your mind and there I will be.'

She smiled at me so serenely
That a wave of peace covered me completely.
I felt at ease all my cares washed away
She brought me renewed hope from that very day.
Now whenever I feel overburdened with pressure
My angel's face I picture and treasure.
I know she's there with her arms around me,
Which helps me smile and feel more carefree,
Ready to face all my struggles ahead,
I remember well all those words she said.

*Sharon Grimer*

## I'M WAITING

I've left you several messages and yet there's no reply
I thought the date went quite well so now I'm wondering why
I made my special curry, it's something I often cook
I know you really loved it because you gave me a tear-filled look
And the wine stain isn't permanent that I made upon your rug
Red wine can wash out easily just by giving it a rub
You said bondage was a good idea but perhaps in retrospect
I shouldn't have swallowed the little key that unlocked the handcuff set
The candle wax I drizzled on you is supposed to be all right
I truly did not mean to set your chest hairs alight
So I hope it's not the firemen that's the reason for no call
I'm sure they didn't mean it by saying, 'Now we've seen it all.'
Wait, maybe you're not out of hospital and you're sitting all alone
I know, I'll get the phone book and give the ward a phone.

*Jill Sunter*

## UNWANTED

Her ice tongue,
I could not melt it, though I tried,
my emotions of fear and anguish, I turned to strength.
It was that strength that pulled me through.

The adoptive mother of a child of three,
her ice tongue ran through the halls of my mind.
'You were too old for me to hold.'
'I never really wanted you.'
And I remember the picture, which I had now found,
of my birth mother, she was holding me on her knee.

The adoptive mother her ice tongue cut me through.
My life began with a colour,
the colour of ice blue.

I had been so cold and lonely,
my mind built a wonderland in the acres of land of new home.
The magic of the fairies as they dressed the trees,
with a breath of ice snow,
my white castle glow.

When the ice-cold droplets of water were caught in time,
it filled my mind,
like glistening capsules hung on trees.

When the fairy winds cast their ice hands,
they made magic wonderlands,
that was where this child was happy to be.

Cutting through it all, though I was so small,
was her ice tongue telling me she never really wanted me,
but it felt right, here at my fairy winter tree.

They cast their ice hands, and there fell a blanket of glow.
My real mother, again I will know!

*M A Cahill*

## MY SNOWMAN

As a youngster I loved playing in the deep snow.
It turned a grimy industrial town
in Manchester UK into a winter wonderland.
If I desired to build a snowman
I would start off with a small snow ball
and would roll it along the snowy ground
until it had grown into an enormous ball.
With a little carving and few additions
such as coal for eyes, nose and mouth,
I had made an edifice of a healthy man of snow.
The icy reality remained for a few days,
he never grumbled or moaned about anything.
But as the temperature rose,
the penniless snowman dissolved from sight.
Where had he gone? And; will he ever return?
Ah! the thoughts of a child.
Of course; my individual snowman
will not come back in the identical style in which I constructed him.
But, every year, in many countries of the world
innovative snowmen are modelled.
They too will evaporate and go back to the agreeable status of nature,
into the lodgings my original snowman now resides.

The next time you visit the beach or a park pond,
take a deep concentrated look inside the flowing motion of the water
and see if you can chance upon my snowman,
fidgeting in the reflection of the midday sun.

*Michael Levy*

## CHANGE AND CONTROLLED CHANGE

An expeditious and harsh family split,
Resulted to part of the family, living in a dirty bed sit.
From a quiet town, to a home in the hectic city,
Unfamiliar surroundings and without Dad was a pity.
A new step-dad, violent and a controlling lover,
Created catastrophic events and a bitter mother
Who projected her fear and rage towards her innocent child,
Who was smitten by Mum's dark persona, now callous and wild.
When the child was of age, she fled from the hostile home,
Although free from aggravation, she was isolated from siblings
                                        and alone.
This unsettling lifestyle interfered with her education,
And various ill health problems were solved through
                                    prescribed medication.
With extremely high expectations to succeed in life,
And a need to feel worthy and achieve, despite much strife.
Determination and persistence earned her a well-deserved degree,
                                        held with pride,
Which gave much confidence and a new self-love,
With strength to push the past aside.

*Michelle White*

## LIFE OF A PHOTOGRAPH

I send a photograph to my grandson, aged six:
an exciting image of the fastest vehicle on earth,
he is impressed, shows it to his parents and friends,
he saves it carefully with others in a drawer,
over the years from time to time he looks at it,
his life changes through adolescence and beyond,
the photographs move with him from place to place,
some are thrown away for lack of sustained interest,
the one from his grandfather retains his loyalty,
from time to time over the years he looks at it,
he sees the news about other high-powered vehicles
which surpass the land-speed record he remembers,
the photograph recalls a mere moment of history,
it makes little impression on his son, aged six,
over the speeding years he rarely remembers it,
while inertia protects it from being discarded,
the death of his grandfather fades from his memory,
the picture holds no interest for his grandson.

At his death, age-old sentiment comes to an end,
like all other items of purely personal interest
the meaningless photograph is finally disposed of.

*Neville Davis*

## OVERTAKEN BY A STRANGER

A stranger overtook them in their walk
That night in spring, on the Emmaus Road,
And as they walked they felt the need to talk,
And tell him of their great heart-crushing load.

When they reached Emmaus a warming glow
Stirred their hearts within them, and they both said
He should stay the night - but they did not know
He was the Lord, until He broke the bread!

He overtakes us as life's way we tread,
And walks with us on our Emmaus Road . . .
On our dark hearts His radiant light is shed,
Straightens our back, and shares each heavy load.

Invite strangers in to sit at your board . . .
When one breaks your bread you may see the Lord!

*Dan Pugh*

# MRS DIMPLY DEE

Deep in the heart of the forest in a cave big and rare
Lived Daddy Bear, Mummy Bear and little Bruno Bear
Bruno was a happy bear who liked to have fun
His mummy and daddy loved their little son
Not far was he allowed to roam from the safety of his home
Yet one day unnoticed he ran off on his own
Deep into the forest looking for someone to play
On and on he ran laughing all the way
Soon the trees looked taller and the light not very bright
Bruno had not noticed the day had turned to night
Suddenly he stopped and looked around in despair
He could not find his way back to Mummy and Daddy Bear
What a naughty bear he was for not doing as they say
Would he ever find them again and end this scary day
What Bruno did not know sitting high up in a tree
Was a wise old owl called Mrs Dimply Dee
She gave a little hoot and a friendly wink
Bruno told her unhappily, 'I am lost I think.'
Down she flew beside him, 'Now my dear, let me see
Do not be afraid I am Mrs Dimply Dee
Back home I will take you to Mummy and Daddy Bear
Yet run away again don't you ever, ever dare.'
So back home they travelled, through the tall, dark trees
Bruno the bear and Mrs Dimply Dee
The sun came up shining as the day began to dawn
With little Bruno back in his cave safe and warm
He opened his sleepy eyes and cuddled close to Mum
Saying, 'I had a dream last night but it was not fun.'
Yet did this really happen or was it just a dream?
No one will ever know except Mrs Dimply Dee.

*Doreen Biddiscombe*

## A WONDERFUL IRISH MAN

He was a friendly Irish man
full of charm and jokes,
very possessive and proud
of his dearly loved folk.

I loved him so clearly
because he's my dad
He was the best friend
I ever had.

He guided me with love
through the pitfalls of life.
Now he's taken a journey
to see his loving wife.

Both of them now together,
sharing their love and smiles.
One day I will see them again
safe from the world's trials.

*Julie Brown*

# HOLOCAUST

Thrown in the truck - despite their mother's pleas
Young victims of Nazi atrocities -
Four children torn from Mother's caring side
To take the truck of no return's death ride.
She begged the guard to set her children free
With frenzied screams convulsed in agony -
Wild piercing screams that no one could ignore
To haunt all silent moments evermore.

She struck the guard - fists tight in manic blows,
His words fell cold while terror-struck, she froze.
'Take one,' he said, 'you may take only one!'
A dreadful quandary had just begun.
Eight little hands stretched out, 'Take me! Take me!'
Four little faces racked in misery.
Eight flooding wells of tears in soulful trust,
While she, in turmoil, stricken, writhed nonplussed.

Which one? Which one? she sobbed, I have to choose -
Three of my precious children I must lose.
Which one? Which one? I have to choose just one!
Then suddenly she saw the truck was gone.
Her outstretched arms were empty as she fell
Drowning in tears that time alone could quell.
Eight little hands she knew she'd always see -
Eight little hands stretched out imploringly.

*Joy Saunders*

## THE JOHN GILBERT

Nestled in the trees and in the lee
Of the tall spired church of Worsley
Stands a new pub in English tradition
Providing the locals with spiritual addition.
The Parson's Nose was the first name ventured
But this suggestion was quickly censured
So the John Gilbert was aptly named
After the man who was famed
As the agent for the Duke of Bridgewater
Who built the canal as a cheap transporter
Of coal of Manchester in 1761
Which raised prosperity for everyone.
The Duke's old gatehouse, not razed to the ground
Forms part of the pub because it was sound
So like the phoenix from the ashes
The building grew in delightful flashes
Of architectural verve and vision
With beautiful lines of aesthetic precision.
No featureless structure of steel and glass
But honeyed stone of elegant class
Nor box-like shape all flat and square
But nooks and crannies with artistic flare.
Clustered chimneys reach for the sky
That stand like sentinels and lead the eye
To intricate ridges on steep roof lines
And curved cornices that combines
To create a blind of picturesque unity
With nature and the close vicinity.
Now John Gilbert can rest in his grave
Content that Old England is partly saved.

*Bill Newham*

## GLOBAL WARNING

We sat holding hands creating a conclave,
summoning pagan forces for the waters to spring.

Shrivelled frogs blinked with croaks of disapproval
at our disturbance of their parched domain,
dismayed by our grip on fanciful hopes.

The sludge of our scepticism rose inert
revealing our disdain of manifest signs
buried in Delphic sands.

We kissed the moisture of our lips
making love as the only tangible fact
of drowning in sensual oblivion.

The breath of our bodies brought embers
to flare, joining seminal juices
into the flow of loving

spiralling upward to light the reality
of our survival in an impenetrable void.

*Michael Fenton*

## FOR TRUDE

The estancia -
Landscape of sunlight and grass
For the wild horses.

The tero-teros,
Emus and armadillos
Roamed free as the air,

Despite the gauchos
With knives slitting the lambs' throats
As innocence wept.

The breeze stirred the grass
As we rode the savannah,
Sky full of white birds.

You and Erico
Escaped the worse blood-letting
Of the Holocaust

And, wrenched from your roots,
Proclaimed paradise your own,
A new creation.

Like an aureole,
You spread light, replenishing
The world's granary.

Now you are unwell,
We send you our love, praying
That the wild horses

Bring you protection
While the tero-teros sing
Sweetest lullabies.

May sunshine warm you
As the wind sweeps the pampas
And tall grasses bend.

*Norman Bissett*

# A SMALL CANNON BALL

Walking on Fowey foreshore I found
A small cannon ball fired from a 'drake' I am told.
(A 'drake' being a small and manoeuvrable cannon)
    But no less deadly than a full-sized round.

    It sounds a clarion call down through time.
    Who lit the torch, the French or one of us?
    One of us I'm told or in 1644
    One of them, the King's men
    If you were on this side.
    This side of the river, a Parliamentarian.
    No room for cross-benchers then.

        A small cannon ball
    It invokes the smell of gunpowder
                and the stench of fear.
    The cries of pain and the gunner's cheer.
    The power to maim and widows make.

    Innocently it sits nicely in my palm.
    Harmless now, when once,
    It could neatly have taken off my arm.

    Sitting on the table it is no cause for alarm.
A mute reminder that, Cain and Abel were only the first.
    And Charles the first was not the last.
    The time for killing isn't past.

*Jack Major*

# A WONDERFUL LIFE

She had everything she wanted,
A big house and a car,
Success she had achieved,
She had come very far,

She'd worked hard all of her life,
She'd met a charming man,
She had two lovely children,
It was all part of her plan.

She'd travelled far and wide,
Holidays in the sun,
Expensive meals, hotels,
She'd had her share of fun.

She'd lived well, but she'd been careful,
She never overdid it,
She resisted cigarettes,
The odd drink, she never hid it.

But suddenly she felt tired,
And now she had a pain,
She saw doctors, had a test,
Her life was going down the drain.

It was time for her to suffer,
She bravely smiled and said,
'I've loved every minute of my life,
Remember me when I'm dead.'

*June Melbourn*

# THE CAT HOME

I want a cat to call my own
And give it love and
A brand new home

But how can I choose
There's such a lot
I'll have a ginger tom
Or maybe not

Then out sprang a little gem
She was white and brown
And black again

What can I choose
They're all so nice
Will it be Ginger or Sooty
Or little mixed spice

I think I'll go and ask the vet
And then I spied my perfect pet

She was snowy white
With big green eyes
She sprang on my lap
And purred and cried

I knew she was the one
As she sat upon my knee
She'll spend the rest of her life
Content and living free.

*Marilyn Davidson*

## FIDELITY

*Tick-tock*, a glance at the clock . . .

You will be knocking on the door,
right now. I know you won't be late.
Did you shine your shoes,
scrub behind your ears?

Tut. Just listen to me - as if you
were a little lad, or I a mad mother!

But you are a peacemaker;
and he an 80-year-old.
I recall how he attended
my mother's funeral,
arriving halfway through.
She deserved so much more.

Such disrespect brought such distress;
my silence sealed for twenty years.
But it is too late for hate.
Life is not forever.

But blood is bonding.
A strength in solitude.

You and I learned too soon,
that life, like diamonds -
lasts not forever.

Yet, when all else is lost, love lives . . .

*Anita Richards*

# THE CREATURES' GREAT GUITAR SOLO

Step into my parlour
Said the spider to the fly
But he turned down temptation
And he kept on soaring high
Thank you for your invitation
But I have to turn you down
For there's something big going on out here
And I'm planning to stick around

Now come into my garden
Said the flower to the bee
Well I'm sorry to disappoint you
Although you're tempting me
But there's something big going on out here
That I've just got to see

Then in the distance they both heard
The music being played
And everything from everywhere
Began to make their way
To a place where creatures came
Oh from near and far
To listen to a lone man
Playing on his lead guitar

(Chorus)
Now they all sat and listened
Yes they all took it in
Swayed to the music
And began to sing
Well doesn't it feel just groovy?
Doesn't it feel just right?
As they all gathered hands
And danced into the night

Now in the distance as more head
The music being played
Well they all rose to their feet
And began to make their way
To a place where creatures came
Yes from near and far
To listen to a lone man
Playing on his lead guitar

(Chorus)

So it's the story of the spider
Who couldn't tempt the fly?
The bee who didn't land in the flower
No he kept on soaring high
The story of the creatures
Who came from near and far
To listen to a lone man
Playing on his lead guitar
The story of the creatures
Who came from near and far
To listen to a lone man
Playing on his lead guitar.

***Darren Morgan***

# THE BALLAD OF MEG KNOCKEEN

Come listen, good people, I'll tell you a story
of a broth of a woman, her name Meg Knockeen.
Though old when I knew her, her black hair grown hoary,
she was yet brave and comely and walked like a queen,
for the queen of her village she was in her youth
and her beauty was such you'd walk miles to have seen;
and the lads that were wooing her only spoke truth
when they swore, 'There's no equal to dark Meg Knockeen.'

Black Patrick Muldoon said he'd ne'er wed another,
and promised all rivals he'd tear them apart;
Red Seumas O'Leary too caused her much bother,
but slim, gentle, fair Willy Flynn had her heart.

Then the Black one and Red one lay waiting for Willy,
they caught him and beat him till life fled away,
threw him into the river that brawled by Meg's cabin,
she found her dead love there at dawn of the day.

She wept not nor spoke until Willy was buried,
then said to the murderers in strange empty voice,
'Well, seeing as you're both so keen to be married
I've thought of a way to decide on my choice.
You must fight on the bridge and the one who wins over
shall be married to me by good Father Mulqueen!'
So up with your fists, boys, good luck to the lover
who wins for a bride the dark Meg Knockeen.

Then grimly they fought on the worn wooden bridge boards
soon slippery with blood from the combatants twain
till Seumas the Red made a desperate lunge towards
his foe, slipped and fell and was ne'er seen again.
For the torrent ran fierce on that morning, they say,
and swift bore his body a-down to the sea,
but, beneath the triumphant one, boards broke away,
the wild waters claimed him and dark Meg stood free

But later, men found, when they mended the bridge span
that the boards had been weakened with axe strokes and fire.
'Small wonder,' they said, ' that the weight of that one man
was finally more than the strained planks could bear.'

They looked at each other but no word was spoken,
for all knew as clearly as if they had seen,
'twas the work of a woman whose heart had been broken.
Willy Flynn lay avenged by his dark Meg Knockeen.

*Josephine Offord*

# HUH! HUH!

I once knew a most unusual chap,
Whose features were like an old relief map.
He had no teeth and was covered in fur:
At birth he was christened Mr Ben Hur.

He couldn't count and he couldn't write,
But still he was thought to be very bright.
He walked on his hands and sat on his feet,
Which was where his ears were inclined to meet.

He went to school but he came home again -
Ben couldn't get on with his fountain pen.
When he learned to swear on an abacus,
He didn't know why they made such a fuss.

So then he stopped learning altogether,
And got a job forecasting the weather.
He started riding thoroughbred horses
In figure eights on Jockey Club courses.

He also drove chariots with great élan
As he banged away on a frying pan.
There were fifty sharp knives of Sheffield Steel
Sticking right out from the side of each wheel.

He scared all his foes and all his friends too,
Who scurried away and hid in a loo.
The air raid warden wielded his rattle,
Which frightened himself as well as cattle.

Ben Hur was condemned by all at UN,
And told that he mustn't do it again.
He changed his name from Ben Hur to Herr Ben,
Which caused people to ask, 'Wer ist das denn?'

*Ken Cox*

## TEENAGE MOTHER

This picture is grim,
I feel so alone.
I'm scared and cold
I wish I was home.

Two babies to look after,
What am I to do.
When I think, what
I put my children through.

My heart is breaking,
I start to cry.
I punish myself
I want to die.

Outside the snow is falling,
Inside the walls are wet.
No heat, no food,
I've slipped right through the net.

God looked down,
Placed an angel by my side.
He must have done that for me
Because we all survived.

*J Lowe*

## WAITING FOR PERCY

I'm waiting for Percy
Each day I'm here
I hear his call
But he never comes near
He knows that I'm waiting
Hours at a time
And when I'm not looking
He'll swoop in and sit on the line

He's a wood pigeon, Percy to me
And he plays little games with me
But this Yorkshire terrier
Is brave and bold
And patient, so I've been told
So I'll keep on waiting
And I'll bide my time
For one day his tail feather
Will be mine, all mine.

*A D Cartledge*

## 'TWAS ON AN APRIL MORNING

'Twas on an April morning,
Just as the day was dawning,
I came upon a maiden, fair,
With eyes so blue and golden hair,
Who looked at me with tear-stained cheeks
And said, 'I've had no food for weeks.
My ma and pa have thrown me out.
They have their reasons, I've no doubt,
But Sir, I really crave a meal
Of bread and cheese, or cooked cowheel.'
I said, 'Then please come home with me
For breakfast and a pot of tea.
I need a maid to clean my house;
A housekeeper, one day a spouse.'
'Oh Sir, I know you not at all.
Though you are handsome, strong and tall,
You might just want me for your bed.
Who knows what thoughts run through your head?'
'Well, suit yourself.' All I could say,
'And starve, my girl.' Then walked away.

*Joyce Walker*

## CHASING THE WORM

The afternoon was hot, the sun was high in the sky,
And an ocean of warm rays filtered down, reached Miguel and I.
As we basked like two whales in the afternoon heat
We decided there and then to embark on a journey,
As had many before, for we were two foolish men.
We had to start at the top we decided, and make our way to the end,
We took deep breaths, and then we began, we would not yield or bend.

We would follow the worm, chase the Cusano Rojo,
From the summit we would descend,
Two men with nothing better to do,
We would see it through to the end.
Miguel took the plunge, with a smile on his face,
I saw him take a deep swallow,
And I, in all truth, with no hesitation, wasn't far behind to follow.
We knew it would not be easy, for this trail we had followed before,
Only to end ingloriously, both stretched out upon the floor.

The way was easy to begin with, as we followed the golden trail,
Determined we both to see it through,
Resolved that this time we would not fail.
A third of the way gone, we were fine, we thought,
The worm still led us on,
And we swallowed some more, we were doing just fine,
As we toiled in the heat of the sun.
Just over halfway, the end in sight,
This son of Oaxaca could be defeated,
But our eyes were starting to blur a little,
A sense of time slowly retreated.

We swallowed and gulped, we were almost there,
The bottom could clearly be seen,
And Miguel and I laughed at the worm,
Which looked to us quite miserable and mean.
It was harder by now to concentrate,
My hands had lost their co-ordination,
Miguel was looking quite green, I suppose I did too,
As we lost control of the situation.
The worm was winning again I knew,
As I slumped backwards in my chair,
My hat fell to the ground, my head exposed to the sun,
And somehow I didn't care.

Miguel tried to rise, but his legs wouldn't work,
So he sat with a smile on his face,
The worm just floated in the golden sea,
I thought it had a big grin on its face.
We knew we wouldn't get to the end,
A whole bottle was just too much,
So we slumped in our chairs, and let sleep take us both,
After all, we were in no rush.
One day, I thought, as my eyes clouded over,
In my drink-induced golden haze,
One day the whole bottle of Mezcal we'd devour,
Maybe one of these days . . .

(Famous for the floating worm in each bottle,
Mezcal is a strong alcoholic beverage
Made from the pulp of the agave cactus.)

*Juan Pablo Jalisco*

# A SUMMER DAY

I awoke to the sound of soft, gentle waves lapping the sandy shore
and the music they made as they swished back over the shingle at
the water's edge. Rising from my cosy bed, I parted the curtains.
The gold light of dawn was gleaming on the skyline, paving a path to
the clear blue sky, promising a day of unbroken sunshine.

My feet sank into the cool, soft sand that trickled through my
bare toes, leaving my footprints invisible, as if they had never been.
I sensed a slight tremor of apprehension, the excitement of a new
beginning, a new day.

The sun rose steadily, at first pleasantly warm, a whisper of a breeze
caressing my face, then increasingly became a still, unrelenting heat
as it climbed in the sky. Suddenly, as if by some magnetic force, my
whole being became alive, sensing an awareness beyond my control,
drawn towards a vision of manhood, a Greek Adonis, tall, fair,
bronzed, rippling muscles glistening in the sun; alone, oblivious to
sound or sight, fathomless, deep blue eyes electrifying a spark into a
flame of unbridled passion, an excitement, an ecstasy, that ebbed
and flowed in the heat of emotional madness.

Blissful sleep, dreams in exquisite contrast! Tranquillity in wooded
countryside, light and shadow playing through the leaves, creating a
dappled carpet on the earth below, a meandering stream gurgling by
my feet and cool evening breezes ruffling my hair - a delightful scene
created by nature. A dream, a fantasy, reality - who can tell?

Once more the cool, soft sand trickling through my toes the music
of the waves . . . ?

*Dorothy Kemp*

# LITTLE HAROLD

Harold was an orphan he'd just turned ten years old,
He'd always been a caution his friends said he was bold.

But, really Harold was lonely he longed for a mum and dad
It's all he ever wanted, only they all reckoned he was bad

He tried to do the right thing but his efforts all went wrong,
He tried his best to fit right in, but could never get along.

They would all take him back again, saying he was far too old
For them to teach him, then to train, they couldn't break the mould.

Poor young Harold's heart would ache he just couldn't understand,
Why no one could be bothered to take the trouble to hold his hand.

Back at the orphanage, he would land, the unhappy little lad
Then something happened, quite unplanned that made him very glad.

A lovely letter came to say she had travelled very far
That she would take him home today and would travel there by car.

Now she, was his grandmother, one he never knew he had,
Who happened to be the mother of his late beloved dad.

The letter said, that she'd just found that Harold had existed.
It was a shock, but they were bound to get along,
His granny had insisted.

Little Harold got so excited he took a voluntary bath,
He really was delighted when complimented by the staff.

At last the hour had arrived, his granny came to collect him,
He wasn't sure how he survived, or why this lady should select him.

When at last he saw her, his heart began to leap frog,
For there, standing before her was the sweetest little dog.

Home is where the heart is and this little dog had stole his heart,
Granny said her home was part his, now his brand new life could start.

*Valerie McKinley*

## VIAJE DE LOS LLANEROS
### *(Drover's journey)*

All the cattle are moaning inside the corrals,
Not a harmonious sound, more a symphony from hell.
Dawn is just breaking the long journey must start,
Making late preparations as we wait to depart.
Tame oxen in position outside the large yards
A 'half moon' of cowboys spread like a pack of cards.
My horse 'Patalejo' has good cattle sense
His strong muscles beneath me impatient and tense.
I give the signal and gates fly wide,
A surge of dusty confusion - it's the start of the drive.
Our mounts all a jitter the herd charge our way,
Whips cracking, men shouting, we hold them at bay,
All one thousand head are milling around,
Great exertion to settle them as hooves hammer the ground.
All are steady now ready to move on,
Flank riders positioned and 'point' starts his song . . .
'Vamos Novillos' his voice carries well,
The herd starts to follow the tone, like a bell.
Our journey will take us way across the plains,
To the edge of the jungle lush with wet season rains.

Stretched far out now in long formation,
Cattle under control no 'maverick' breaks station.
A mere dot in the distance 'point' continues to sing,
The sound floating back like a heavenly hymn.
The men covering the rear are lost in a cloud,
As dust flying high obscures like a shroud.
At the bank of the river herd and horses quench thirst,
Trying to cross the swift current we stumble and curse.
Out of the water all hides dripping wet
We gather formation, our destination is set.
We slouch in the saddle as the sun climbs high,
No shade from the heat and no clouds in the sky.
Shouts and thundering hooves! as a steer breaks away . . .
Hot pursuit is successful, back on track we stay.

The sun is now sinking, journey's end is in sight,
Men and cattle relax in the cool of the night.
After a meal and a drink we sit in the sand
I reflect on my thoughts of this wild and wonderful land.

**William Moyle Breton**

# BOURNEMOUTH, WISH I WAS THERE

Dreaming
Being on my own
Feet up high
All alone

Miles of
Golden, glittering sand
The beach
Glass of wine in my hand

A lonely toast
To the cliffs,
To the coast

A roaring speech
To Bournemouth
To the beach
For love - for the sun
For joy, for the fun

We've shared through the years
Cheers for laughter
Cheers for tears,
The horizon, the sea
Cheers to you
Cheers to me

As my speech comes to an end
I whisper:
'Please, forever be my friend!'

Just to tell you I care
Good old Bournemouth
I wish I was there

*Jorunn Ingebrigtsen*

## WANTON PASSION

With such elegant style
Sure a stone she'd beguile
And you'd never suspect for a moment
With Janice so cool, surely nobody's fool
Underneath she's in smouldering torment.

*Chorus*
Chocolates, milky or plain
By the slab or the box of selection Milk Tray
Seem to addle her brain.
She's a slave to her passions they say.

Janice tried in a fashion
To cut down her ration,
It ended in shameful disaster
For sad to relate, she got in such a state,
Her compulsions she never could master.

So at work she's reviled
For obsession so wild,
People know of her shameful condition.
She's ensnared as a slave with no pride left to save,
She's possessed by her awful addiction.

I suspected she might be,
I thought at first sight she
Could be a tad query anaemic.
But I now can attest, with a blood sugar test
We've discovered she's hypoglycaemic.

So those friends who despise her,
Should now re-appraise her.
She's not an undisciplined glutton
When Jan's in a spin, it's just her insulin
That is pressing her chocolate button!

*Patrick Brady*

# THE SAILOR DROWNS

*(In memory of Denis Pentaleev. When his ship was in Falmouth he would meet his friends from the Seamen's Missions)*

The reaching seas join distant shores;
A sailor's arms link port to port.
The breath of friendship flows between.

The theatre's full; the stage is set;
The lights come up. Let the show begin;
But deadly actors lurk in the wings.

The actors of death have taken the stage;
The audience gripped by a drama of fear.
Hostages taken; a random set.

Fifty-six hours of hell have passed.
Freeing forces storm the house,
With shouts and shots and sleeping-gas.

Choking, retching, gasping for breath,
The sailor drowns in a sea of fumes.

*129 hostages died.*

**John Jenkin**

## ROAMING VAGABOND

Through country lanes, a creaking wheel
Signals from beyond the grave,
Memories of a timeless era
Of a traveller oh so brave.
Weather-beaten, he smiled as he sang.
The old grey horse seemed content.
No acknowledgement as they passed,
A vision heaven sent!
Roaming the hills and dales
A country myth, unless you see
His caravan of colours bright,
Parked under a greenwood tree!
A cooking pot over an open fire
Deliciously announces rabbit stew.
Talked about by many,
But observed by very few!
The locals smile and nod their heads,
As you recount your tale.
And yet the camera that you used,
Why did it simply fail?
A century has passed, some say,
Perhaps you were blessed indeed.
To have seen them oh so clearly,
The roaming vagabond and his steed!

*T G Bloodworth*

# THE GATE

I hope in vain, with tempered ear,
The sound to dry the glistening tear
But somehow know I will not hear
The scraping of the gate.

Ill-fitting gate in time-warped frame,
Each time it opens, just the same,
Has been like that since first I came.
One day I'll fix that gate.

This place beside the flowing Nile
Has been my home for quite a while.
Maybe you'll come and see my style
Behind that wooden gate.

I hear your hand upon the latch,
I check my dress is up to scratch.
*At last,* I think, *our lives we'll patch,*
*Together through the gate.*

I must pretend it's no surprise
To let you see, it is not wise,
The light that glows within my eyes.
'When will you mend that gate?'

You play me at my own sweet game,
Pretending that, in truth, you came
With no real motive that you name,
Remarking on the gate.

There really is a scraping noise,
Reality my dream destroys.
'Sabbah Al Khier,' a voice says, 'Kwoiz?'*
Mohammed shuts the gate.

* Arabic: Good morning! Are you well?

*John Belcher*

# WORDS ARE EASY - LIKE THE WIND

I wonder, what sort of story that line could begin?
A story of a gentle wind caressing flowers on a sunny day
Or a hurricane which destroys everything in its way?
Words, people telling a different story every day.
Some cruel, vicious words that can have a price to pay.

Words are easy like the wind.
Now I'm thinking, could that line a story begin,
That portrays words and wind as twins?

There's zephyr
A gentle wind coaxing leaves from trees on an autumn day,
Or a soothing word that gives comfort to someone along life's way.

Tornado - violent, destructive, bringing havoc anywhere,
A spiteful, hurtful word, spoken by someone who never cares.

Mistral, sirocco - can these winds and words be twins? Maybe not.
They remind me of household taps, cold and hot.

Now the wind has been with us since the start of time.
It's been given many descriptions by mankind.

The wind can be similar to a word whispered in one's ear,
Or a noisy outburst, stating a gale is near.

Words are easy like the wind,
Still not sure if a story with that line I could begin,
For a while the wind is moving so easy over land and sea.

I'm pondering- how to pen words of something that,
I cannot see.

*J A Booth*

# PRISONER OF THE PAST

She had been his prisoner for many years now.
Unable to break the spell he had cast.
Men had come to release her but their hearts were not true.
Each time one failed the spell grew stronger.
He was sure she would remain his.
Her eyes though could see beyond the walls.
A vision of a true hero.
A man not interested in fame or fortune.
In her mind she called to him and willed him to hear.
The forest hut was sheltered but he heard her all the same.
She had been in his head for longer than he could say.
Packing his axe he set off for the palace.
The old man sensed him and was filled with dread.
This was one that he had not counted on.
The gates opened even though the gatekeeper had the key.
She smiled and the old man dragged her away.
In his head he followed her directions and was at last at the door.
It could not withstand the power of the axe and exploded.
The old man stood firm but his spell was dying.
As the axe swung she fell to her knees.
He rushed to her side and held her.
The spell was broken and her tears flowed.
Evil had been destroyed and now freedom was hers.
He understood her past and never pushed.
Remaining forever her faithful hero and deepest love.

*Anne-Marie Pratt*

# THE SNOOTY CAT
*(With acknowledgements to Carmenarose Burmese)*

I went to see a friend one day
Who said: 'You just might see
My kittens I have bought to breed;
They've a wondrous pedigree.'

I went with her to see the cats.
All four were friendly, wee
And really very well-behaved,
Like folk of quality.

As I was playing with these four
What should I chance to see
But yet another cat, the pet
Of the friend I came to see.

But this black cat, she simply stared.
She turned her back on me.
She turned her nose up; it was plain
She had no pedigree.

*Jillian Mounter*

## OUR NANNY

Rain showing picturesque patterns on
windows, showing patterns like tears.
Little hands trying to erase them but
they were outside, not in.
Children locked into the nursery
with Nanny the tyrant.
'Come on you children, your meal is ready.'
Grumbling, the children sit to eat.
No playing outside today.
'Eat up, then find a toy to play with
for that rain is here to stay.
No sunshine today my lovelies.'
How the children yearn for the sun
to shine again, to gleam on the panes.
Next day great joy, as Nanny said
the magic words, 'Put on your coats.'
They look, the rainbows are shining
on the now rather dirty glass windows.
Reaching the park they feel not cold,
warmly clad in coats, scarves and mittens.
They rush to the swings, slides, roundabouts.
The sun is not hot but it seems like a heatwave
for they can play outside again today.
Nanny, no tyrant, just the one they love.

*Marj Busby*

# WHO KNOWS?

He lies cold and waxen without breath,
His eyelids closed, his actions stilled.
His words of criticism frozen in his brain.
He has no power now he's been killed.

I'm wrong! His power still lingers.
He left a will, his money might buy
A revenge from Hell. His eldest son can't point a finger
Or find the guilty guy.

He and his brothers stare down at the coffin,
The priest prays, the brothers make vows.
The widow cries and the crows watch
Until they feel safe to fly from the boughs . . .

Of the swaying dark trees. Gloom descends
On the mourners, they shake with fear.
Which one of them killed this mean old man?
He'd raped four children, all so dear . . .

Two innocent angels of my son, John and Min
Who lived next door to this evil man.
The more I think, the more I groan
As the anger grows. I sure as can . . .

Save Ellie, my wife, from being found out
As the one who drew blood, she struck with a knife
At his heart, which couldn't have been there.
But the stab wound ended his life.

I clutch my chest, the pain I feel
Is hard to bear, as I leave the Earth.
Poor Ellie will be alone. I fall and kneel.
She looks and screams for all she's worth.

My Ellie . . . God! Help her . . .

*Sylvia Scoville*

## A MODERN PARABLE

For Gerthrude all that had gone before
Was one long bloody civil war.
A Berundi widow in great need
No food for her young kids to feed.

But with her neighbours they walked tall
Towards the church for help for all,
And to their joy a loan perceived
No money but ten goats received.

Now Gerthrude's children had milk each day
Their health got better in every way,
The goats they also provided manure
Which improved the soil fertility sure.

The fertile soil gave a higher yield
As Gerthrude cultivated her field,
Now her family could have food
Indeed her way of life improved.

The surplus crops she did not need
She sold for other mouths to feed,
The extra cash for education
A time of thanks and meditation.

Now the ten goats, ten kids they bore
And in other years there would be more,
But the first ten kids the loan repaid
Were then recycled by Christian Aid.

Now Gerthrude's flock has grown indeed
And she no longer is in need,
Yet you will agree with me I'm sure
How one small loan can help the poor.

*David A Garside*

# A JOURNEY TOO FAR

'Good evening to you. Take care on the roads.
Deep snow is widespread and hazardous now.'
No comfort was felt from these parting words;
My thoughts viewed with dread the journey to come:
Weather changed landmarks, road narrow with bends -
Seldom in use on more temperate days.

White flakes swirled around as wipers worked hard
To keep spaces clear on ice-coated glass.
My car slid off course. Shock hit me in waves
As remedies tried did not halt the skid.
Menacing shapes of hoar hedges beckoned;
With eyes tightly shut, I headed their way.

*Is this my end?* My anxious thoughts questioned
Whilst force-tortured metal groaned and ploughed on.
Then all movement ceased. Taped music played on.
I still felt alive. Closed eyes opened up.
Tight neck and shoulders unwound from their hunch;
I struggled and fought to squeeze my way out.

Silence surrounded my shivering form.
Some time elapsed as I peered up the track.
Two headlights appeared, came down towards me.
A landrover slowly drew alongside.
Deep voice through its window offered a tow.
My Triumph was saved by a work-clothed knight.

Bright lights from my home shone out a welcome;
Conversation and food steadied my nerves.
Comfort and warmth enticed me to linger;
Wise husband that night had other ideas.
My poor battered car was pressed into use
And driven by me along the same route.

*E Joan Knight*

# WHY?

The loss so hard to bear
Wrenched hearts, total despair
So much expected joy, gone with anguished cries
Why? We question why?

Holding hands looking at the evening sky
We see a star shining bright
We seek each other's eyes, sadness within our hearts
We walk inside, our first but not our last

We have no answers
Our lives are changed, outwardly we are the same
Mysteries may not unfold until we are very old
We must be strong to carry on, a light will shine
And maybe then we can move on

A star twinkling in the sky is watching over Mama and Papa
When moments of joy open our hearts once more
We'll look to the sky and remember, but with new eyes

*Meg Mitchell*

## IN A DARKER WORLD

A growing boy
the world began to close
around him everywhere.
Blindness not just a pose

Still he pretended
he could see
where'er he went in sun or rain
o'er fen or lea

The walls closed in.
He nowhere went
a trick he played on friends
from his adolescent tent

A man he is now
sure in his constraint of blindness
too proud to pretend.
No use for kindness

The world's his stage
to act out his affliction
like a habit. The complaint
'tis his benediction

Flowers he can smell
from his dark prison
they tie him to the good earth,
the least frisson:

A wider birth
into a world of senses grey.
Life is fine-tuned in the dark.
It nothing takes away.

***Angus Richmond***

## THE BREAD KNIFE

An antique knife for cutting bread
With 'Firpo's' sculptured in the handle
And on the blade a similar patter
'Firpo's' of Calcutta
Will you kindly pass the butter.

I often wondered where it came from
I found it in a caravan
Did it come from a colonial
Or an Indian restaurant man?

Then one day I met a lady - grand dame of the British raj
'Please pass the butter - not the marg!'
She knew of 'Firpo's' in an instant
With great excitement she recalled
A famous restaurant in Calcutta
Which manufactured chocolate bars.

I heard they had an orchestra
That played for all the diners
The scene was grand and colourful
With service of the finest.

My bread knife has a special warmth
When now I grasp the handle
And pictures of a bygone age
Flash by of Indian grandeur.

*Elizabeth Cleveland*

# EVERY POEM TELLS A STORY - A MIRACLE?

The pastor's kitten was stuck up a tree
And she wouldn't come down at all,
The priest, somehow, had to find a way
Or else she might have a bad fall.

A brilliant idea came to his mind
And he tied a rope to the tree,
Then attached it securely to his car,
'This is the answer,' said he.

He began driving slowly away
Till the branches were really bent,
Boing! Suddenly the rope broke
And the kitten through the air was sent.

Later he went out shopping,
Saw a woman who hated cats,
But her basket was full of their food -
Had she got one for chasing some rats?

Her little girl had wanted a cat
But her mum had always said no,
Unless she prayed to God for one
It was never likely to show.

Out in the garden the child knelt down
And then - what did occur?
A kitten came flying through the air
And landed in front of her!

The child was delighted,
The mother was amazed,
The pastor was overcome with joy
As on his kitten he gazed.

*Rita Hardiman*

# WIND IN MY HAIR, SUN ON MY FACE

Wind in my hair
sun on my face,
as I board the ferry to a place,
I had never seen,
full of fear, full of joy,
as I walked round I could
see that place I was to call
home for a time,
my soul was full of joy and
of unknowing as it docked
with my bag of dreams,
as time passed, I found my
feet and was to meet folks from
all walks of life, some I would
have walked by in my everyday
life back home,
but I was to work and live with
them, and grew to call them my
friends; some I'll meet again, some
I won't. One thing I know, I'll never
forget them and I wish them well
in all that they do.
A summer of fun, joy, love and most
of all happiness and friendships that
will never end.
When I left I took with me lessons in
life that will change me for the better,
all thanks to the folks that made that
happen on the Isle of Arran 2003.

*Kirsty Keane*

# THE NAVIGATIONAL CANAL

This canal was once a dream, for men that had a vision,
In the past years, which was part of a scheme
They knew that as they toiled to move the stone and dig the soil
Time would tell to future beings these men had worked hard to
                                                make a dream come true

So today it seems a sin
That we have let the canals drain off
And get filled with rubbish and tins
The very system that once kept men in jobs and a country
Also allowed them to make a bob
As I travel along the banks I see what could be and give thanks
All the hard work is covered up with bramble trees and shrubs
But with vision and hard work, it need not be a gamble
For to bring back its former glory
Can be done to tell a story
Of our heritage and men so bold, we can tell that story to our children
When we go grey
And grow old.

*Toby*

# EGYPT

No country ever can compare with Egypt; land of wealthy kings.
Its pyramids in timeless state - once held treasures of wondrous things.
The sphinx that guards the pharaoh's tomb; an effigy of man and beast.
To view these wonders of the world, our admiration can never cease.

Massive statues of pharaohs' past; are there to see on desert sand.
Carvings worked upon this stone will tell us of this ancient land.
Hieroglyphics and paintings show the stories of this exalted race.
Colour lingers on clothes they wore; beauty still on a queenly face.

Where the river Nile flows, transforming all to a holy scene
The farmers and the oxen there tend the land a fertile green.
As this lifeline wends its way we see upon the delta shore,
The grandeur of the temples there, Karnak, Amon and Luxor.
As they catch the evening sun, changing all to coral red.
Such beauty we can only stare, no words are needed to be said.
Wandering these columned halls, our stature dwarfed by towering stone
We marvel that this edifice was made by man and man alone.

In the Valley of the Kings, where buried lies the royal tombs,
Murals still as beautiful are hidden in descending rooms.
Musicians playing to their gods amidst a painted sky of blue,
Hidden for three thousand years, colours still as bright in hue.
The pharaoh, King Tutankamun, in his capsulated seal,
When discovered in royal state, once loosened, did at last reveal
The immensity and awesome sight of turquoise, gold and ebonite.
A bejewelled throne and gilded cask, the wonder of the golden mask
Unparalleled - this beauteous thing; the bounty of an Egyptian king.

***Molly Phasey***

# THOUGHTS OF FREELAND NOW

The rain falls like the tears of God
Tears of sorrow, of things I once had
I sit in the churchyard and think of the pain
Of the lives of all the people here lain
The village has changed so very much
Shop closed, post office and such
Children's happy voices as they race from school
When grown up they will leave, I'm no fool
Houses for sale, sadness fills the air
Why is it like this? Doesn't anyone care?
The strong wind blows my hair, trying to say
Nothing is the same as it was yesterday
I have so many memories of this special place
But all I can see takes the smile from my face
Traffic whizzes past at lightning speed
All that people want seem to speak of greed
I return to the convent where there is peace
Where I can escape, momentarily at least
The tulip tree still stands tall and serene
Seems to say it understands what's gone between
I miss the creaky chairs, clock that ticked too loud
The cast iron bath with legs that stuck out proud
Rooms with only lino, no heat to keep you warm
All this spoke of poverty, but had a special charm
No dishwasher then, you used the kitchen sink
So many, many changes really makes you think
Lighten up, I tell myself, you can't live in the past
But what surrounds me now - I just can't grasp
One thing however fills my heart with praise
My Saviour never changes, no matter how the days

*Veronica Quainton*

# STRANGERS IN THE NIGHT

So he woke up,
Faced the black of the night.
His heart pounding,
Like thunder in the sky.
Sweat pouring down,
Like rain in a flood.
Blood-stained sheets,
And on the table a gun.

Incidents like lightning,
Flashing in the night.
He felt the pain,
Remembered the violence.
Screams echo,
Unheard in his mind.
The body lay next to him,
Cold as ice.

Beds creaking,
Lovers dancing in the night.
Flies bathe in red,
Blood dripping on the ground.
Rain hammers down,
Sweat crawling down the wall.
He sings to her,
Bloodied footprints on the floor.

Her blonde hair,
Crimson in the light,
Tears streaming down his face,
His mind in freefall.
Tries to wash away his sins,
Their blood mingles as it falls,
Strangers in the night,
They'd never met before.

*Kevin O'Gorman*

# ONCE UPON A TIME

Once upon a time a beetle named Potter
lived with his wife, three sons and a daughter,
deep in the earth where the sun never got to.
The years passed by and one day, father John
said to his lad, John Potterson One,
'Son, go out in the world and learn
the wisdom and skill of foreign land.'
His son went forward with much delight
and was not gone long when he espied
a maiden in a waterfall playing with a golden ball.
She was so beautiful, lithesome and tall
and her ball was so prettily made out of gold,
that Mr John Potterson was totally smitten with her.
'Would you prefer to get married now or later?'
he asked her as soon as he could.
'Good Sir, if I could marry you I would,'
she replied, 'but I'm a prisoner of the spider
who lives beside this babbling brook.'
'Fear not, fair maid,' said the brave potter's son,
'when I've slaughtered the spider we'll marry anon.'
The spider, however, was bigger than John,
with long, hairy legs and a poisonous tongue,
and when it got wind of what John had to say,
it leapt over the maiden and whisked him away.

*Jackie Davey*

## THE AMERICAN DREAM

A typical middle-aged American sits reading,
Wearing a pullover, white shirt and fawn slacks.
Thoughts streaming; in part day dreaming,
And feeling completely relaxed,
Seemingly untaxed by worldly woes.
He savours the words in the paperback he's reading,
Holds them briefly, then lets them go.
So comfortable in his easy chair,
Feeling blameless, without a care.
'God is good!' to himself declares
As someone else's dream he reads.
A frown, a smile, this is all he needs, he thinks,
At least just for a while.
Such pleasure he is gleaning,
He fails to notice I invade the scene.
This seems a very 50s picture show.
Me, impinging on his living space,
Of this perfect, friendly American male.
What tale does he have to tell
Of his war in the South Pacific?
A 2nd World War hero and survivor,
Fighting the Japs around Java's coast.
The war won thanks in part to Uncle Sam.
The Korean War short-lived, now gone.
Economy booming; guys outside pruning,
Or immaculately grooming their front lawn.
Polishing their Chryslers, living the American dream
Yet a cold-war shadow sometimes shades the sun.

*Jonathan Pegg*

## THE NAME'S THE SAME

The stranger in Llanbetws
Stuck out like snow in Hell
Dark he was and saturnine
Full sinister as well.

The post master was all polite
Whilst listening to his plea,
'I need to contact one Dai Jones
To rendezvous with me.'

'Just bide a bit, I'll telephone,'
No sooner said than done
He rang the man and then explained
Dai'd meet him prompt at one.

The chap arrived, the stranger bent
And whispered in his ear.
'The swallows fly low this summer
Be brave and show no fear.'

'But I am Dai Jones, butcher,'
The villager winked his eye,
'The fellow that you really want
Is Dai Jones, the secret spy.'

*Sarah Blackmore*

# THE VASE

Twelve inches high: Derby, Chelsea or Bow?
Death passes it to nearest relation.
And each new owner would put it on show,
Till it went to the next generation.

It passed to a banker named Henry Hood.
Then the finest porcelain shared its shelf.
But soon the treasures among which it stood
Were sold off because of declining wealth.

But proudly it stayed on the mantelpiece.
Its position by a marble-cased clock.
When Hood's daughter died it passed to her niece,
A middle-aged spinster, Miss Mary Brock.

Then Miss Brock died without making a will.
Nephews and nieces were her next of kin.
They were Brenda and Bert, Betty and Bill;
And Michael and Maisie, Maurice and Min.

Who should inherit? They could not decide.
A nephew then coughed, a niece blew her nose.
They all wanted it: the youngest girl cried.
An elderly woman sniffed at a rose.

They chose an umpire to settle dispute,
Who suggested putting names in a hat.
(He looked very smart in his brown striped suit.)
But not one of them would agree to that.

No concern for its history, its beauty,
Was displayed by the nephews and nieces.
Just greed. Arbiter then did his duty:
He smashed the vase and shared out the pieces.

Some might think that he had made a mistake.
But he laughed: he knew this vase was a fake.

*F G Ward*

## THE SHED

Fred got up one morning and went to mend his shed
As he bent down to get the nails
A plank fell on his head
So he jumped back to dodge out of the way
And stood on a rake instead
The rake flipped back and hit his face
With lots of force and might
Poor Fred it gave him such a shock
He yelled out loud with fright
And as he yelled, the cat ran out
Which gave him quite a scare
Now he fell down and hurt his back
Upon a broken chair
By now Fred's aching quite a bit
His face has got a nasty tic
He gets up slowly to walk out the door
And catches his toe on a brick
As he falls down, he falls real hard
On top of his wheelbarrow
Which in turn, turns upside down
Upon Fred's best prize marrow
By now he's feeling black and blue
And no nearer mending his shed
'I should have known better to start this job
I wish I'd stayed in bed.'

*Christine Corby*

# IN THE SPACE OF TIME

In the midst of time we are suspended,
And time moves forward with or without us,
We each have a place in the open space,
Every breath we breathe is a gift of grace.

In childhood bliss we thrived with love,
Taking goodness for granted as children would,
But the bubble can burst at any time,
When it does - we're enlightened, and we survive.

At every stage of growing up, freedom calls us,
To have our own way, do our own thing, regardless,
It's a never-ending struggle that drives us on,
We learn from home, at school, and having fun.

At an early age we are given choices,
Responsibility weighs heavy, but freedom rejoices,
If we get it wrong we may have regrets,
But we can learn for ourselves how to pass the test.

There is more to life than personal needs,
To live life to the full, we need friends who agree,
We all have gifts to use and to share with others,
As God's children we have many sisters and brothers.

When we think we know all that is said and done,
We find it's the simple things in life that mattered all along,
When the young-hearted old and the thriving young,
Can level with each other as one to one.

*Kathleen McBurney*

## THE LAKE OF MENTEITH

Oh Menteith, cold water laps they shore
The heater bends in torture o'er the lea,
Ever crying, 'Amata, where is she?'
'Twas from thy tangled, icy depth they bore
Her lifeless body to the hapless shore.
Oh! What a dole of woe, what bitter tears.
Oh! What a cry of pain, what broken vows
Before the holocaust, her spirit bows -
And breaks against the emptiness of years
The lonely desperation of her fears.
'Twas for precious love, she her vows forsook
Yet ere she dropped her veil and called his name
Master of Menteith, a deed of evil blame
All bloody black with treachery o'ertook -
That happy lord, singing his way by brook
And leafy fern, winging his way to love
From hidden place dire treachery out leaped
A clash of steel, till was the heather steeped
Crimson with his blood, nor Heaven above
Could avert his fate, or his foe men move
'A priest for Jesus sake, my soul is fled.'
'Twas that false Judas came commiserate
To his sins, that black degenerate
He believing the beloved safe from dread,
Calling love's sweet name ere he was dead.
Oh! Menteith, cold water laps thy shore.
Wailing, wailing, Amata evermore.
The heather bends in torture o'er the lea,
Ever crying, 'Amata, where is she?'

*B Kerby*

# IN NEED OF SOME ACTION

The first time I hit this town was on a grey day in LA
The people looked jaded and the architecture looked like it
needed reassuring
Hell, I needed some action

I headed downtown, via the subway with the rest of the mob.
The guys looked like stiffs in a hurry on the run from a rob
Hell, I needed some action

My throat was dry and I fancied a drink,
But the bars were all shut and I needed to think
Hell, I needed some action

There was only one thing to do, I'd go shoot some pool,
But the pool was closed and the firearms were under wraps
'Bummer!'

My nerves were tingling, this place was not cool
I had to extricate myself, I was nobody's fool
Hell, I needed some action

I passed a drugstore, the radio was on
The voice blasted my airways
It was loud, clear and strong

It said, 'As reports confirmed earlier,
The hurricane heading for our town
Changed course in the last hour and went off on its own

However, another hurricane known as 'Harry'
One of the biggest to hit the States
Is headed our way at an alarming rate.'

God I had to get out of this place
Hell, this *was* the action
And I didn't need it . . .

*Janice Honeybourne*

## MARTIAN DREAMS
*(For Danielle love Nanna)*

One dark September night
When bats caught moths in frantic flight
Shone a planet big and bold
Containing secrets to be told
Mars was the planet's name
As closer and closer to Earth it came
Everybody stopped and stared
Counted stars and then compared
And wondered if there's life up there.
Who thought of Earth and would they care?
Care to meet the folk in town
And how would they travel down?
In a big round flying dish?
Or something narrow like a fish?
With flashing lights and playing tunes
Symbols carved like ancient runes
Blown by fast winds in a stream
Sliding down a moonlight beam
Martian men in suits of green
Like no one here has ever seen
Or reddish-brown just like rust
From fighting through the layers of dust
With carbon dioxide in their air
Would they bring us some to share
In buckets of fizzy lemonade
Shouting folks, it's all fresh made
Then darkness faded into dawn
People sighed then did yawn
As off they wandered to their beds
With dreams of spaceships in their heads.

*Angela Edwards*

## DREAMER

Dreamer is a creature
And quite a mixture
Made up of feathers and dust
Loves to be tickled, but only just

If you can catch him
A speed of ten light years
Friends skiddy and strim
Their bodies of honeycomb and white curly ears

Toffee island is a place where they live
Interesting clouds are made of sugar almonds
Plenty of candy and iced cake to give
Out of his sky, to Earth, falls pink spiralled sticks to the ground

A banana split they take a glide
To the next space station, which is named Tizzy
Splish and Splash are water aliens, waiting to go to tide
Dreamer and his mates get off the split really quizzy

Singing and very happy all together
Looking over at the two aliens, Splish and Splash
Because the two of them were Pi and Pirp Squash
It's thirsty, travelling, zooming around Tweather

Coming towards us a flying spaceship
It was trying to make us fall off the station
So we got hold of Twinks, to rescue us, with a hop and a skip
Twinks is a fuzz-ball from Ink, he was saved by restoration

The station is held together with chewing gum
Rolling around and playing, having fun
Now we are near complete, a wizard named Screamer
Kept calling again and again, in sleep, wake up you dreamer.

*Jan Ross*

# OUT OF EDEN (ALL THE STARS OUR STAGE)

Did mankind from out of Eden come?
Emerging from the jungle into hot African sun.
Adam, from his ape ancestors made his great escape.
Step by faltering step, evolving into the human race
At what stage did he question, what he did see?
To consider the wonder of his surroundings.
The God in the heart of you and me.
Did Eve stand steadfastly by his side?
As across the grassy plains they did boldly stride
Into the African heartland, they quizzically gazed around,
As the great beasts of the veldt in untold numbers grazed.
And when put to flight, in their might, shook the ground.
Did these new human creatures live in constant fear
As packs and prides of savage carnivores drew near?
What we know is their numbers slowly grew.
From Eden's keepers, these palpable precious few,
Until they outgrew the land of their birth,
Spreading forth to fill all the corners of the Earth.
Far from the dirt from whence they sprang.
To briefly flare in the open air; have their existence,
Until they returned back to their sacred land.
So far from their forefathers their seeds did multiply,
Until their descendants by and by,
Crossed the seven seas and filled the lands,
And then sought another goal, reaching for the sky.
Now we, born of ancestral Adam, in our present age,
At the night-time heavens upwardly we gaze,
And say, above is our true destination,
For is not today, all the stars our stage?

*Julia Pegg*

# CAUTION - MEN AT WORK!

George Bush once had a shocking dream and woke up with an
awful scream
He dreamt that hour after hour his planes had bombed a foreign power.
This dream it caused George great dismay, more like a nightmare you
might say,
For on behalf of Uncle Sam he'd meant to bomb that chap Saddam
But all his planes had gone astray, some this-a-way, some that-a-way,
Instead of heading for Iraq they'd gone to Africa and back.
What's more, each plane contained a load, not of smart bombs
primed to explode,
But of big parcels  and sweet cards which read, 'From George, with
kind regards'!
And so bold pilots without fear dropped cookies over Tanzania,
And pecan pie fell without harm on places like Dar-es-Salaam.
And where Bush goes, I always find, our Tony Blair's not far behind,
Thus soon an SAS commander was dropping rissoles on Rwanda,
The RAF spread tripe across Botswana and scattered cottage loaves
in Ghana
Air commodores with shiny pips bombarded Chad with fish and chips!
The Congo people changed their ways and ate Caerphilly cheese
for days,
Malawi stalwarts when they could, tucked into beef and Yorkshire pud.
Both Bush and Blair were mortified, they sat around and sulked
and sighed,
They said, 'We can go on no more, let's send for Duncan Smith
and Gore.'
But soon to Bush and Blair's surprise they both received the
Nobel Prize,
And then despite a few complaints the Pope, God bless him, made
them saints!
Said Bush and Blair, now saints so true, (and being politicians too!)
'Food for the starving can't be bad, beats bombing kids in
old Baghdad!'

*Peter Davies*

# TIME LAPSE

I tell a tale both chilling and dark
which, believe it or not
is true. I was sitting alone in the park,
it was noon, and hot.
A young, pregnant woman walked by and asked
to share my seat.
Unwillingly I agreed, and together we basked
in the sun. The heat
as intense and yet she seemed icily cold
and, to my surprise,
turned suddenly toward me and asked how old
I was. Her eyes
burned through me. 'Old enough,' I said,
'to have fathered you.'
'Are you married?' she asked. I shook my head
though knowing she somehow knew.
'Your mother died giving birth to a child,'
she said. I started!
How could she know? She sighed, then smiled
and, saying no more, departed.
That night, alone and unable to sleep
I searched high and low
till I'd found, in the long-hidden box where I keep
mementoes of long ago,
the photo of her, who, as I child, I should mourn
but never see,
that is, until today, in the park, with her unborn
child - me!

*Alan Millard*

# NATURE LOVER

Will thee walk with me sweet love,
Let's tread nature's paths together.
Through the corn of burnished gold,
Along the silver jewel that is the river.
Beneath majestic forest pines
Amid the bonnie purple heather.

Will we steal a kiss, sweet love, and
Will I hear thee speak my name
In some enchanted fairy dell,
Where autumn leaves have turned to flame?
We can wander where we choose, throw off all the ties that bind us,
Like wandering vagabonds, leaving sorrows far behind us.

Will thee lie with me, sweet love,
And soothe the aching heart of a dreamer
Beside the crystal waterfall, and see how swift it tumbles over?
See the downy mountain dew, nestle o'er the fields of clover.
For it's thee that I adore, and I'll forsake thee never,
I will love thee - till all the earth stands still,
Until the end of ever.

*Jilly Tynan*

## CHILDHOOD MEMORIES

The blue sparkling sea
Waits for you and me,
Crabs scurry away
On this sunny day.
Seaweed gaily flowing,
Breezes gently blowing,
Solitary beaches
Covered by tide's reaches.
Silvery half-hidden shells,
Memory within us knells
Of a place forever changing,
Land that water's rearranging.
Filling up our moats and castles
Built throughout by earls and vassals;
Walls so thick and turrets wide
They are all claimed by the tide.
Even us, so tall and strong
Cannot face the sea headlong.
So build your castles while you may
For they'll have vanished by next day.

*Linda Cooper*

# STANDING UNDER A PURPLE UMBRELLA

Forced out into the rain by addiction
I entered a park bare of humankind.
I stood beside deep crimson berries
ripened on bushes, circled with
flurried leaves tossing and falling to
their withering end.

Four steps in front my imagination
captured a lake with scenery of rocks
and prairies standing close, a fisherman's
solitude broken with the catch of the day
with fish springing to taste our world.
Reality was a puddle of water with raindrops
making waves, splashing my shoes.

As I held my shield from the spraying
waterfall a darkness fell hard but
my skin shone luminous rays
down to my feet, a melted red and blue.
With my need fulfilled and dampened,
I looked at the beauty of the rain and smiled;
I was standing under a purple umbrella.

*Suzzette Goddard*

## OUTCAST

Uncomfortably crude
for upwardly mobile neighbours,
your threadbare home cowers lonely
in field's corner.

Read one-time self respect
in careful capitals of its name,
sign now reeling drunkenly, like
you too often.

Your old dog nothing cares
for their disdain, companion
of a decade's toil, and play that cheers
your solitude.

But, like sudden sunlight
on a snowbound scene, friendliness
awakes a toothless smile for those who
can't despise you -

remembering your arm,
once strong, tended the rose that gives
to passers-by a draught of its
crimson sweetness.

*Elinor Wilson*

## JOURNEYS

I sat on the train from London to Glasgow
And passed not a word with anyone there
Halfway through the journey
I took all my clothes off
If anyone naoticed
I wasn't aware.

I sat on a train from Rome down to Naples
And learnt the life history of everyone there
Ate bread and salami
With a lady from Bari
A man from Perugia
Sang a song from Paliacci
And babies were crying
And people were laughing
And a man from Cattania
Whose wife had just left him
Was telling his tale
To the lady from Bari
Who knew about life
And was so understanding -

When the train stopped in Naples
I wasn't aware.

*Nicolette Turner*

# HOW I WISH I WAS HER!

The sun beats down on the playground, five years old
and the world is ours.
School photos today, we smile, with teeth not quite there
sticky sweets to blame who cares!
My friend sits wriggling on a chair, I giggle as I watch, her
pretty face, her beautiful chestnut hair.
How I wish I was her!

Time goes by and lives are altered.
She broke my doll today but I never faltered.
The friend I had now pulls my hair,
She makes fun of me but I just don't care.
How I wish I was her!

The years go by and new friendships are made.
We make now friends but the memories don't fade.
The boys just love her sleek new figure,
Everything about her just got bigger.
How I wish I was her!

It's time for marriage and for babies -
Twenty years go by it seems like ages.
One day the ringing phone makes my life worthwhile.
It's her! I have to smile the memories never faded.
We're going to meet, I hope I don't look jaded.
How I wish I was her!

Now our lives have come full circle
From Infant's school to married life.
She has no husband, but I'm a wife.
How I wish I was her!

*Christine Gibson*

## SCOTCH MIST

The symbol of Scotland
and so the thistle begins,
a tale of a legend
that blew in the winds.
Of a man who would sit over locking Loch Ness,
from the rise of dew mornings
till the sunset no less.

Telling his stories crafted by hand,
on folks and the mystery's on remote Scottish lands.
His words overflowing on paper pen glides,
a man named McStewart and the treasure he hides.

Bagpipes laying on his worn sporran and kilt,
as he talks to the dark murky waters like silk.
Then his music lifts through the snow-bitten sky,
with Nessie the monster as their duet echoes high.

So beneath the coolness of his watery lair,
where Nessie's wee lassie and their family still share.
Living off haggis and whisky home brewed,
his favourite diet of scones and broth stew.

Then as legend holds a ship wrecked off the coast,
McStewart and Nessie borrowed its teak, gold locked chest.
Dragging it over rough cliff and beach coves,
opening it when the tide and light low.

Slips through their fingers pieces silver and gold,
papers unfolded being of tatty ripped scrolls.
Maps and a letter from a giant to a maid,
of the causeway he built so to romance her each day.

But as gusts of winds whip over the mystery of Loch Ness
so the treasure now lost and McStewart's myth
of Nessie that lives beneath this own quiet rest.

*A A Murphy*

# MY SWEET SPRING

Don't wait too long to open your eyes,
This cold - this dankness I despise -
These lazy days are not my tune.
Oh please spring - do come soon.

Do come soon - I mope - I swoon,
In wintry darkest gloom.
I know behind the grey you're there
But while I wait I feel despair.

I dream of the golden glint on a mare,
A hopping - poppin' marching hare.
My ears are alive to the sound of binds,
The sweetest music I have heard.

Milky snowdrops glow like a pearl,
Babbling brooks - they swish and swirl.
A child will dance in the fairy ring,
Oh please come - my sweet spring.

*Wendy Watkin*

# THE BALLAD OF BOOKHAM COMMON

*(A true story of how we came to buy The White House
named after Mr White)*

Only three months from our wedding,
With a baby on the way,
Our small flat we must be shedding,
For a house we'd have to pay.

Lying on St Tropez's beaches,
Stupid in the midday sun,
My wife reads The Lady's pages,
'Here I've got the perfect one!'

'Twenty-five miles out of London,
A cottage with a little land,
On the edge of Bookham Common,
Ideal for retirement and . . .'

'Can we see it when we get back?'
'If you wish, dear,' said the Drone.
Little dreaming, when exhausted,
What he'd find, when he got home!

'We'll have to rush, if we're to find it,
I said we'd be there before dark,
It isn't far from Bookham Station,
So we'll need no time to park.'

It was a perfect April evening,
After rain the sky was clear,
We found our little country cottage,
Two thousand pounds, it wasn't dear!

Seven years I commuted,
Ninety minutes door to door,
While we changed the country cottage.
You'd not know it any more!

Four years to get electric power!
(Water and phone already there)
Four children came to show them our
Determination, make them care!

We still had that country cottage,
When at last we did retire,
But for us it was not perfect,
To bigger things we did aspire!

***Patrick Davies***

# THE COTSWOLDS

The beauty of the Cotswolds
Are the walls all built of stone
Villages and towns a must to
Visit and roam.

The rivers running through them
An old mill or two
The beauty of the landscape
From the hills to view.

Walking in the country lanes
They're full of things to see
Rabbits darting through the
Hedges, into the fields they flee.

Pussy willow hanging so graceful
From the trees, wild primroses
And daffodils, blowing gently
In the breeze.

The farmer on his tractor
Ploughing furrows straight and true.
The cattle start towards the gate
As the milking time is due.

As the clouds meet overhead
It's time to head for home
For tomorrow I'll be here,
The Cotswolds for to roam.

*Beryl Smyter*

## EVE

All we ever wanted was a baby of our own,
to make our life complete, to make our house a home.
Finally it happened - in my womb you grew
and we counted down the minutes to the date that you were due.
We were longing just to see you, and at last our time it came,
just knowing soon I'd hold you, kept me smiling through the pain.
You made a silent entry into a noisy world
and I heard your father shouting, 'It's a little baby girl.'
But you were whisked away before I had a chance to see;
they said that you were very ill; took you away from me.
Later I did hold you, and my tears splashed on your head,
but you would never feel them, my poor baby girl was dead.
So we've named you for the grandma, I never got to know,
we hope that she will watch you, in the place that you now go.
Our love and prayers go with you, as we lay you in the ground;
our darling baby Eve, who came and went without a sound.

*Bonita Hall*

# THE TINY SHEPHERD

The tiny shepherd saw the star
And heard the angels singing.
And, while the others stood in awe,
His little feet were winging
Down hill, through vale across the town,
With childish joy unheeding,
Straight up to the manger cradle
As though a hand were leading,
To halt his excitements rush
Where the newborn babe is sleeping.

How sweet to see the innocence
Awake at gentle peeping!
As tiny hand clasps tiny hand
Eyes smile at touching tender,
'Ere long there melts a young boy's heart
In absolute surrender.

Long before the older ones
Had reasoned what to do.
The little shepherd's open heart
Had sped, because he knew
With the unerring instinct
And trust of simple things,
That the babe the angels sang
Was for him the King of Kings.

*Cecilia M Monk*

## ONLY A GAME

I will always remember Nellie,
And our vibrant, childhood days.
Never quite, knowing what to expect,
With her wild and willful ways.
She was part of a large family
And I felt sorry for her,
For she was the runt of the litter
Yet treated, more like the cur!
She played on my softer emotions
So long her antics I bore.
I grew tired of being her mentor
And told her, I'd take no more.
She tried to make light of my protest
As always, denying blame.
With her get out phrase as usual,
'Come on, it's only a game!'
She told me she was moving away
And appealed for sympathy,
I told her that I no longer cared
Then I walked away, feeling free!
On the day I was told that she'd died
I cried a river of tears.
For I knew I'd carried ill feelings
Like a child, for many years.
I went to the woods where as children
She and I had often played,
A posy of bluebells I gathered
Then upon her grave I laid.
I stood there alone in the churchyard
In anguish I called out her name.
I'm sorry Nellie, please forgive me
For it was only a game!

*Patricia Whittle*

# THE VALLEY OF THE SHADOW

The sun's rose-madder eye brings its nightly close,
life-force biorhythms fade as daylight folds
holding life at this defining moment in calm equipoise,
smoothing the white waters of its tumultuous course.

Climbing these cold windswept funnelled passes
narrowing to thread-like tunnelled arteries,
time lengthens between in-drawn breath and deed,
it begins - the slow reduction of death's bride.

Rock faces frown upon a deeply shadowed valley,
birds chatter as they roost on darkened ledges,
safe while these outcrops host their night-time lodges.
But Death's raven stays awake, perched in the nearby gully.

A changeling cradling: the once damned-up streams
swell in the springtime rains, salving deep scars in old murrains;
tumbling to make lagoons of the arid lowland plains,
where I refill my own blue lake of slumbering dreams.

Fazed senses falter like an ignited Catherine wheel
slowing, slowing, as it spirals to predestined oblivion:
the blackened centre alone remains, now a womb-dark icon;
expiring with a last in-drawn sigh and earthward fall.

Something drags at my feet so that I skid towards the precipice;
by some strange power the darting eye's abstracted stare
alert to danger is bypassed: the familiar governance of fear
overthrown as life's restraining ties unbind - and all is peace.

I drift among rosy clouds shrouding foreboding mountain peaks,
smaller than the swarming insects, a speck of dust of no significance.
Beyond the far distant horizon is my destiny where dark matter waits:
do you not hear its muted call, those whispered cosmic sibilants?

I hitch a ride across the Great Divide on a fiery blazing comet
awaiting to connect me with my guardian mountain spirit.
She is my re-birth consort, guiding me on that glorious highway,
midwife and mentor, leading me to His enlightening skyway!

*Norman Meadows*

# THE FISH THAT CAME FOR DINNER

We took a fish out to dinner
We conversed with the trout for a while
There was something real fishy about him
When he beamed the mean fish smile
We ordered some cokes for the gathering
And the trout gave another wry smile
Then he jumped into his drink, with a nasty wink
This creature so terribly vile
And at the main course, may I point out
His manners were so unrefined
He slithered around in his gray scaly gown
And blew air bubbles into the wine
This sea creature needed a lickin'
He sure was no aristofish
I said it was time that we all did some thinking
We thought of a wonderful dish
Dad held him up, while I knocked him out cold
It was just like a Parthian shot
Then we loaded in spices, and other surprises
And cooked him in the pot
We watched with wide eyes, until he was done
This mean and formidable fish
And now feel no pity for as you may guess
He made quite a sumptuous dish!

*Nicole Braganza*

# REASON FOR LIVING

Walking in sorrow down a long country lane
I spied a young piebald with a long tatty mane.
I said, 'Pardon me pony have you not got a comb?'
He said, 'Go on your way and just leave me alone!'

I looked at him crossly and said, 'Your manners I hate,
And I don't understand how you got in this state!'
'I was brought by a man whose name it was Zach -
Who said he'd return but her never came back!'

My heart filled with pity and I said, 'Oh come here!'
And I brushed him all over from his head to his rear!
When I was done he raised his head high -
That's when I noticed the tears in his eye!

'Please don't you leave me in this field anymore -
If you just take me with you I'll be yours evermore.'
So I jumped on his back and we rode far away -
And that piebald is with me to this very day!

We live in the shadows of a mountain so high
Where we sit in the evenings and chat him and I
And we count ourselves lucky that we met in that lane -
Where we both found a reason for living again!

*Cora Barras*

## UNFORGIVING LIGHT

The night was humid yet cold
My future about to be foretold
In silent anticipation there I stood
Waiting in the forgotten wood

The shadow came before me first
The thundering sky became a curse
Fragile fingers brushed against strong
I knew now it wouldn't be long.

Deep into the woods, I was led
Not looking back, only ahead
Started to conjure ghostly things
Puppets run by invisible strings

And as they danced in time with us
Their memories open, sinful lust
The black night sky deepening still
The ghostly ghouls about to kill

Further we danced in time
Each step played out a pantomime
Until the end is finally clear
The path has ended, we are here.

*Emma Scott*